The Nuts and Bolts of Teaching Writing

DEDICATION

To Carmen Fariña, Superintendent of Region 8 in New York City, who has shown the world what is possible when school leadership and professional development are absolutely aligned.

FirstHand
An imprint of Heinemann
A division of Reed Elsevier Inc.
361 Hanover Street
Portsmouth, NH 03801-3912
www.heinemann.com

Offices and agents throughout the world

Photography: Peter Cunningham

Rubrics and checklists adapted by permission from *New Standards*. The *New Standards*® assessment system includes performance standards with performance descriptions, student work samples and commentaries, on-demand examinations, and a portfolio system. For more information, contact the National Center on Education and the Economy, 202-783-3668 or www.ncee.org.

Library of Congress Cataloging-in-Publication Data

Calkins, Lucy McCormick.
   The nuts and bolts of teaching writing / Lucy Calkins.
   p. cm. — (Units of study for primary writing)
   ISBN 0-325-00579-6 (pbk. : alk. paper)
   1. English language-Composition and exercises-Study and teaching (Primary)—United States. 2. Curriculum planning-United
      States. I. Title.
LB1529.U5C3554 2003   2003019529
372.62'3--dc22

Printed in the United States of America on acid-free paper

07   06   05   ML   4   5

SERIES COMPONENTS

▶ **The Nuts and Bolts of Teaching Writing** provides a comprehensive overview of the processes and structures of the primary writing workshop.

▶ You'll use **The Conferring Handbook** as you work with individual students to identify and address specific writing issues.

▶ The seven **Units of Study**, each covering approximately four weeks of instruction, give you the strategies, lesson plans, and tools you'll need to teach writing to your students in powerful, lasting ways. Presented sequentially, the Units take your children from oral and pictorial story telling, through emergent and into fluent writing.

▶ To support your writing program, the **Resources for Primary Writers CD-ROM** provides video and print resources. You'll find clips of the authors teaching some of the lessons, booklists, supplementary material, **reproducibles**, and **overheads**.

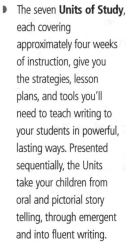

KH

Acknowledgments   iii

Chapter 1 **An Overview**   1

Chapter 2 **Pathways for Writers: "My Children Don't Yet Know Their ABCs. How Can They Write?"**   8

Chapter 3 **Planning Curriculum in a Primary Writing Workshop**   19

Chapter 4 **Managing the Writing Workshop**   28

Chapter 5 **Teaching Methods: Minilessons That Power Your Curriculum**   45

Chapter 6 **Conferring with Young Writers**   61

Chapter 7 **Supporting English Language Learners**   70

Chapter 8 **The Literacy Instruction That Surrounds and Supports the Teaching of Writing**   75

Chapter 9 **Assessment**   83

8/21/05

ACKNOWLEDGMENTS

When I taught second graders, my children and I sang a song that contained the verse:

What do you do when this dream that you have
Is more than a man can build or plan?
You gather your friends from the ends of the earth
To lend a hand in its hour of birth.

For our hands are strong and our hearts are young,
And the dreamer keeps dreamin', ages long.

This series of books turned into a dream that was far bigger than anything I could build or plan on my own, and so I did gather my friends from the ends of the earth. Now that the entire series is almost done, I have a very long thank-you letter to write!

Most of all, I am grateful to my editor and friend, Kate Montgomery. Kate and I have shared responsibility for this series, and we've worked shoulder-to-shoulder on every step and every page. Kate managed the complex interpersonal challenges of a project involving so many people and dimensions, and did so with grace, tact, and good sense. She also led us in what became a groundbreaking effort to imagine and create a whole new genre of writing. Kate never relinquished her principles—believing always in the intelligence of teachers, the importance of writing that sings with clarity and rhythm—and yet she helped me loosen my hold on a narrative form that has served me well over the years. Kate has been my guide, companion, teacher, counselor—and her capacity to work hard has inspired me to do likewise.

Kate did not work alone. I have published many books with Heinemann, and none have received the attentive, thoughtful care that these books have been given. Mike Gibbons has brought his vision for FirstHand to the series and helped us imagine our form and audience. Leigh Peake has rallied us to work in new ways to make this series open pathways that others can follow. Lois Bridges has contributed her wisdom at so many turns of the road. Lisa Fowler and Jean Lawler helped me countless times with the production of the book. I owe thanks to the entire Heinemann team.

I am grateful to each of the co-authors. You will come to know them in the pages of these books and admire them as I do. What you cannot know are the particular roles they played in this endeavor. I am grateful to Natalie Louis; she produced more than her share of the book we co-authored. I am grateful to Abby Oxenhorn; her book was the first one that we wrote, and Abby went on to help with other books as well. I am grateful to Amanda Hartman; *Authors as Mentors* was a challenging book to write, but Amanda was nevertheless up for more and joined me also in writing two tremendously fun books on conferring. Zoë Ryder White, also a co-author on the conferring books, assisted in many of the books as well. I thank Stephanie Parsons for her verve and imagination as a writer and for her willingness to settle for nothing less than our best. I am grateful to Leah Mermelstein for her sterling clarity. Pat Bleichman opened her classroom to me and to all the co-authors, allowing us to learn from her and her children at every step. Linda Chen and Mary Ann Colbert also contributed to the thinking and writing of this series, and their books will soon join these. Randy Bomer helped us have the courage to break into this new genre of writing; Isoke Nia broadened our image of units of study; Kathleen Tolan lent her wisdom; and Marjorie Martinelli was an invaluable contributor as well.

I could not have led an endeavor of this magnitude without the company and support of the leadership team at the Teachers College Reading and Writing Project. I am grateful to Beth Neville, Associate Director and co-author of the CD-ROM of resource material in this series, and Laurie Pessah, Deputy Director of the Teachers College Reading and Writing Project. Laurie and I wrote *Nonfiction* together, and laughed and learned along the way. This is a team of dedicated and brilliant people who work tirelessly for a cause we care about very much.

Tasha Kalista has served as my right hand throughout this entire project. She coordinated co-authors, merged files, e-mailed manuscripts, managed student writing, smoothed feathers, set deadlines, and generally shepherded the entire effort along.

This series is being published just as New York City sets out on an effort to bring balanced literacy in general, and the reading and writing workshop in particular, to every classroom across the city. The series feels especially important to me right now because it is coming out just when New York City is rallying to bring these ideas into thousands and thousands of classrooms. When I started this effort, I worried that providing such detailed descriptions of Monday, Tuesday, and Wednesday in a writing workshop might confine teachers. But now it is clear that the time has come to open wide the doors to our classrooms and let visitors in on our teaching.

I hope this series of books helps thousands of teachers feel that they have been invited to sit in on writing workshops and hear the details of this marvelous form of teaching. In New York City, those teachers will return to their own classrooms, to a city that says, "This is the approach that all children deserve." I am grateful to all the leaders of New York City's schools, but especially to Judy Chin, Superintendent of Region 3, Lucille Swarns, Superintendent of Region 10, Reyes Irizarry, Superintendent of Region 4, Michelle Fratti, Superintendent of Region 7, Irma Zardoya, Superintendent of Region 1, and above all, to Carmen Fariña, Superintendent of Region 8.

It is to Carmen Fariña that this book and this series are dedicated. She has taught me and the entire Project not to be afraid of working in systemic ways and to realize that in the world of schools—as in the world of texts—carefully designed structures combine with detail to create a lasting effect.

AN OVERVIEW

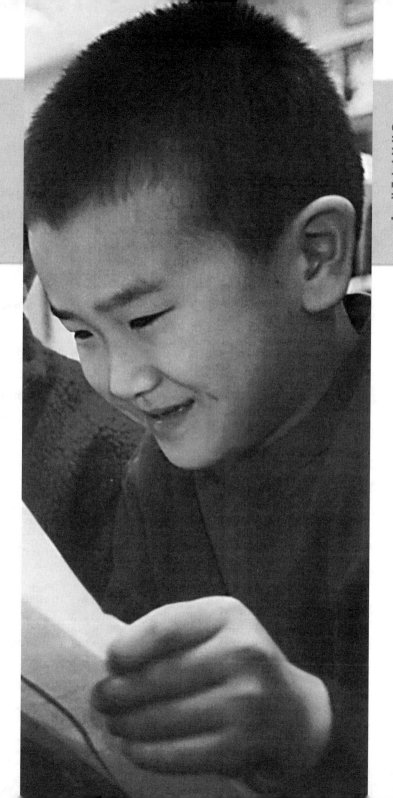

This is the first in a series of books designed to help primary teachers teach a rigorous yearlong writing curriculum. The coauthors of these books and I have helped several hundred thousand teachers make their first forays into the teaching of writing. These teachers have told us that writing has given their children unbelievable power as readers, thinkers, and composers of meaning and that the teaching of writing has given them new energy and joy as teachers, reminding them of why they went into teaching in the first place. We understand what these teachers mean, for writing has done all this and more for us and for our children.

Word has spread. As more and more teachers recognize that the teaching of writing can nourish us and our children, and as it becomes more clear that our children's abilities across many disciplines will be judged through the medium of their writing, the demand for professional development in the teaching of writing has skyrocketed, outstripping our abilities to offer this support. This series of books and the videotapes that accompany it are our effort to hand over what we know so that more children can be given the opportunities they deserve to grow strong as writers and to approach their schooling as makers of knowledge and composers of meaning.

An Overview of the Books

We have written seven books, each of which supports a monthlong (approximately) unit of study in the teaching of writing. The books are organized in a sequence, with each book standing on the shoulders of those that go before it. These books combine to provide the curricular support necessary to take a class of young children on a learning journey. Each book contains the words of our teaching for approximately sixteen days across a unit of study, with suggested ways to extend each of those days if this seems merited. We provide representative examples of the work children did in these units of study, guidelines for conferring with children individually and in small groups, and references to the children's literature that can be a resource during that unit. We detail our goals for each unit and share the assessment rubric that guided our practice and the record keeping we designed to hold us to those goals. We show how all the units of study combine to support children's progress towards the New Primary Standards developed and published by the National Center for Education and the Economy. These rigorous, internationally benchmarked standards have been influential in state standards across the nation, and they are exactly consonant with this curriculum.

Writing instruction happens not only in minilessons but also in conferences. As children tackle new writing challenges, those of us who teach children need to expand our repertoire of ways to confer with them. In *The Conferring Handbook* we tell the story of (and give pointers on) a few conferences that will be especially essential during each unit. For each of these conferences, the crucial and replicable teaching moves have been highlighted. A CD-ROM of reproducibles and videoclips accompanies this series, providing you with sample letters to parents, assessment rubrics, record sheets, and the like. Available separately is a more extensive book on conferring, *Conferring with Primary Writers: Supporting a Month-by-Month Curriculum*. This book contains fifty exemplary conferences as well as guidelines and advice for teachers learning to confer with young writers. Two longer videotapes are also available, showing my colleagues and me working at intervals across the year with the very children and the very lessons you come to know in the books.

Using These Books

In an ideal world, every teacher would have the chance to learn state-of-the-art methods for teaching writing by watching an exemplary teacher instruct her children day to day. Ideally, you would be able to observe these teachers with a coach at your elbow, highlighting the way each day's teaching illustrates a collection of guiding principles and helping you understand alternative decisions the teacher could and could not have made. Although we do not live in an ideal world, these books can be a next-best substitute. They can give you the chance to listen in on and observe our best teaching. As you watch, I will join you on the sidelines as an ever-present coach, highlighting aspects of the teaching that seem especially essential. My goal will be to help you watch any one day's teaching in ways that enable you to extrapolate guidelines and methods that can inform you on another day when you are called on to invent your own teaching.

I know that sometimes you will take the words of our minilessons and bring them verbatim to your own children and that at other times the teaching we describe will need to be altered to fit you and your children. Either way, I know this series of books will keep you company in your teaching of writing and will help you and your children reach new horizons together. The end goal, of course, is not the teaching that we describe but teaching that you, your colleagues, and your children invent together.

An Overview of this Curriculum

In the Teachers College Reading and Writing Project community, planning a writing curriculum is important enough that in the schools with which we work closely, teachers across a grade level spend a full day in June working together with their grade-level colleagues to plan curricular calendars for the upcoming year in both the teaching of reading and of writing. Schools try to devise a schedule so that the teachers across a grade level can meet together several times a week as a support and study group around their anticipated units of study. The projected units of study are usually sent home with parents on Open School Night.

When teachers across a grade level collaborate on the teaching of writing, this provides them with important support. Decades of work in the teaching of writing have convinced me that wise methods of teaching usually do not emerge ex nihilo from a single gifted and talented teacher. Wise methods of teaching do not come from our genes alone but from our communities of practice. Those communities of practice involve not only our colleagues but also teachers who've gone before us. The units of study in these books stand on the shoulders of many communities of teachers, and we hope they provide you with some shoulders on which to stand.

Before we can teach a class of very young children to write, we need to envision the *sort* of work we hope they will do. What can we expect five-year-olds to produce when we ask them to write, and what pathway do we envision they'll travel as they develop? You may ask, "How can my children write? They don't even know their ABCs," and the question is a wise one. As you learn about teaching writing in this series, you'll learn ways to give youngsters training wheels in writing (just as you probably do in reading). With your help, children can travel the world as if they are writers, using whatever they do know to approximate writing while, meanwhile, you provide them with constant opportunities to learn. If children are invited to write each day and if you actively and assertively teach into their best approximations, their development as writers will astonish you, their parents, the school administrators, and best of all, the children themselves.

In order to teach writing, we also need to establish structures that last across every day of our teaching. In this, the first book in the series, I help you establish those structures, and I do so by giving very practical, nitty-gritty advice for room arrangements, materials, expectations, and the like. The wonderful thing about learning to teach writing well is that there are just a few teaching methods that one needs to know and be able to do. I try to provide crystal-clear advice on how to lead efficient and effective minilessons and conferences. I do so knowing that my readers will continue learning about these methods as you travel through the series, encountering dozens of transcripts of each. For now, my emphasis is on the predictable architecture behind all our minilessons and conferences and on the management that allows any of this to be possible. I then overview the yearlong curriculum, nesting it inside a discussion of the standards that inform our teaching and of methods of assessment. I also address concerns I know many of you will have, including a concern for your English language learners.

The yearlong writing curriculum itself is divided into monthlong units of study. Many units of study help children learn to write within a particular genre—say, writing true stories or writing all-about books—and other units highlight particular aspects of the writing process, such as revision or learning from mentor authors. Either way, children generally produce many pieces of writing across a unit of study and then, at the end of the unit, each child selects one or two pieces to revise and edit for publication.

These books assume that in your school, writing is truly regarded as one of the basics. When a school system recognizes that writing is a crucial tool for learning to read and to think across every subject area, then time for writing becomes non-negotiable. This curriculum assumes that K–2 teachers devote at least forty-five minutes (and preferably an hour) a day to instruction in writing. Just as children have opportunities each day to read and to learn math, so, too, they need time each day to write. Writing is far too important to be relegated to the status of busy work, with teachers leading one reading group after another while children write without the benefit of instruction.

In the classrooms described in this series, writing time begins with a minilesson in which teachers offer ten minutes of direct and explicit instruction. After this, children work in highly structured yet responsive environments in order to draft and revise their writing in ways that incorporate the instruction they have received. Teachers, meanwhile, confer with their students individually and in small groups. Midway through the writing time, teachers often call the whole class together for a second teaching point. The day's writing time ends with an opportunity for follow-up with an After the Workshop share about the topic from that day's minilesson.

The teaching of writing relies on other components of the literacy curriculum. It is crucial that teachers read aloud at least several times a day and that some of the texts teachers read (and reread) resemble those that children write. It is important that children study phonics and spelling, learning to build words and to take words apart, to hear their constituent sounds, and to be resourceful word solvers. It is important that the school day includes time for reading to, with, and by children and that children are reading books they can read with confidence, ease, and above all, with comprehension.

Has This Curriculum Been Field Tested?

For almost three decades, the Teachers College Reading and Writing Project has been one of the nation's leading think tanks and providers of professional development in the teaching of writing. Most of the best-selling authors on the teaching of writing were for many years students and/or staff members with the Project. Every summer several thousand teachers attend weeklong institutes with us. The Teachers College Reading and Writing Project works directly and intensely with hundreds of schools across the nation and especially in and around New York City. In most of these schools, every teacher in the school teaches a writing workshop.

The Chancellor of New York City schools recently held a press conference at P.S. 172, a school in which every teacher leads a reading and writing workshop. At the press conference, the Chancellor announced that every child in every New York City school deserves to benefit from a curriculum that matches the one the children at P.S. 172 receive. This means that the writing workshop is being brought to scale in New York City.

The units of study in these books stand on the shoulders of a great many communities of teachers. They have undergone years and years of revision. This curricular calendar existed in oral, hand-me-down fashion for a long while, and as such, has been field tested and revised and refined. Even so, we hope this curricular calendar is regarded not as a script but as a starting point. The community of teachers across a grade level in your school will want to develop curriculum together. In order to devise teaching plans, however, you too will want to stand on the shoulders of other teachers who have gone before you. We hope these books provide you with shoulders on which to stand.

The Authorship of This Series

I co-authored each of these books with a colleague, and the process of writing has been collaborative from long before the moment of inception. Each of the co-authors is either a member of my staff or a teacher I've taught and studied with for years. One of the co-authors, Laurie Pessah, is the Deputy Director of the Teachers College Reading and Writing Project and one, Beth Neville, is Associate Director of the Project. Three of the co-authors are former primary level teachers who are now full-time members of the Project staff (Leah Mermelstein, Amanda Hartman, and Stephanie Parsons), and four are teachers with whom I work especially closely (Abby Oxenhorn and Zoë Ryder White teach kindergarten; Pat Bleichman and Natalie Louis teach first grade).

In primary classrooms, children sometimes work collaboratively on a shared piece. Some call the activity "Share the Pen." The phrase aptly describes the process through which these books have emerged. Although the text reads as if one person gave a minilesson and another transcribed and reflected on it, the process was actually much more collaborative. The coauthors and I began by thinking and learning and planning and drafting teaching ideas together. Then one (and usually several of us) tried out the teaching ideas, usually in many classrooms simultaneously. Based on what we learned, we revised the general ideas, made new plans for the route a unit might travel, and tried those plans in yet more classrooms. Finally we'd feel as if the path was mostly established, and one of us would draft the first few minilessons. Early drafts of minilessons were then passed between the coauthor and me, with the details of the minilessons emerging as we took turns working on them. Once the minilessons were fleshed out, I'd set to work adding other components, starting with the italicized sections. Usually I wrote the introductions and the "Time to Confer," "If You Need More Time," and "Assessment" sections, but sometimes a co-author shared the pen with me.

Kate Montgomery, a former colleague and an acclaimed author, edited the entire series, and her extraordinary contributions are detailed in the acknowledgments.

How Can This Pertain to Kindergarten, First-Grade, and Second-Grade Writers? To English Language Learners?

This series of books chronicles the teaching and learning that occurred in New York City kindergarten and first-grade classrooms. Some of the units were taught in kindergarten or K–1 classrooms, some in first-grade classrooms. One of the classrooms was both an inclusion classroom and a homogeneously grouped class for at-risk learners; another was a classroom in a high-need area. A teacher who reads these books in sequence will notice that the student work in them doesn't improve along a steady upward trajectory; the reason the level of work may seem to regress is that one unit may have been taught in a first grade, the next in a kindergarten! The socioeconomic contexts for the units of study also vary. For example, *Small Moments* is based on a kindergarten, *Writing for Readers* is based on a homogeneous group of at-risk first graders in a challenging socioeconomic setting, and *Revision* chronicles the work of predominantly middle-class first graders.

Although the teaching we describe occurred in kindergarten and first-grade classrooms, we would not have altered instruction had we been teaching second graders rather than K–1 children. This is especially true had we been teaching second graders who had not had the opportunity to participate in this sort of rigorous writing instruction. Writing development relies on and is nourished by prior writing (and reading) experience more than on chronological age.

It is crucial that teachers of kindergarten read the letter I've written to you (see the CD-ROM and page 21) about the ways you can alter this sequence of units just a tiny bit so that it supports your children. Mostly, however, we hope you will trust us enough to realize that although the writing you see in this series may seem beyond what your children can do, the truth is that writing reflects instruction. Your children will dazzle you with what they can do if you give them time each day to write and instructions such as we describe.

These units of study have been developed in New York City classrooms; this means they have been designed for classrooms that contain all the diversity one finds in urban classrooms. A teacher whose class is filled predominantly with English language learners will want to deliberately plan for ways to scaffold children as they rise to the language challenges in this rich curriculum. I've suggested a dozen crucial ways to do this in a section titled "Supporting English Language Learners." The most important thing to say, however, is that this curriculum has provided English language learners with extraordinary support and rich language opportunities.

PATHWAYS FOR WRITERS: "MY CHILDREN DON'T YET KNOW THEIR ABCs. HOW CAN THEY WRITE?"

When we teach writing, we are teaching young people to do something. Whether we are teaching someone to swim or to read, to play the oboe or to write, the *learner* needs to do the bulk of the work. There is very little a teacher can do from the front of the room that will turn someone into a skilled swimmer or oboe player or writer—because the learner needs to do much of the work.

In September, our teaching begins with us sending children off to write and with children proceeding to show us who they are as writers and as people. Once we have invited them to draw things that have happened to them and to write (and tell us) their stories, we will watch closely to see what they do. As we watch and talk with them, we'll learn what our children understand about literacy and what they can do as storytellers, writers, spellers, and readers. As K–2 teachers, we know that we will have a variety of writers in our classroom. We know there will be a range of ability levels from children who can write "squiggles and lollipops" to (perhaps) those who can write pages full of conventional sentences. It is our job to accept this range and to find ways to move each individual toward more and more proficiency.

Children progress in fairly predictable ways from scribbling (in lieu of writing) toward writing extended stories. This means that even before we meet a new class of children, we can already anticipate the learning pathways along which those incoming children will probably travel. When we anticipate the learning pathway, we're more able to move each child along on that journey. Let's look at these pathways in detail.

SOME CHILDREN DRAW AND WRITE AS MOTOR ACTIVITIES

We launch the writing workshop by asking children to think of something important to them and then to draw that on the page. Before the first week of school is over, we will probably see that some children do not try to make drawings that represent meaning. That is, for some children, drawing and writing are motor activities. During the writing workshop, these children are messing around with a pen. One child may fill the page with squiggles, another may make a small mark on one page after another, but either way, when we ask, "Could you tell me about your drawing?" the child will not have a lot to say about the meaning behind the marks. If we press on by asking questions such as, "What's happening in your picture?" these children still won't reveal the meaning their pictures carry. The children will also probably not initiate writing.

How important it will be to help children in this category become immersed in the idea that texts carry messages, that pictures and words hold stories! Our first goal will be to help these children approach the page with an intention to convey meaning. "I like to write about the things I do," I might say. "Don't you? What do you like to do?" If the child answers, "I watch TV," I'll say, "Do you! What do you watch?" If I hear that every morning starts with cereal in front of the cartoons, I will say, "You need to put that here. Draw the bowl of cereal so people will know."

We won't always be present when children draw and write. When children in this category bring us texts that appear to be scribbles, we'll make a special point of assuming that the texts *must* mean something. Pointing to a portion of the child's scrawl, I might ask, "What's happening over here?" Some children will probably invent stories in response to these questions, making their stories long *after* they drew the nonrepresentational marks, and this marks progress. Other children will have actually tried to convey meaning, and my interest will lead them to elaborate on those existing stories by talking and drawing more. My goal will be to ensure that the child's drawings and marks represent meaning for the child, and I won't worry about sound-letter correspondence for a few weeks.

Some Children Convey Meaning in Their Drawings—If They Write at All, It's Unclear What Their Marks Say

Some children will draw in ways that convey meaning. The meaning may not be readily clear to a reader, but if we ask, "Can you tell me the story?" the child has a story to tell. Although the content of the piece may be incoherent and may also be transient, with a new story made to order each time the author rereads the piece, these children nevertheless regard the writing workshop as a time for making meaning.

If there is meaning on the page but it resides only in the drawing, I try to attend to that meaning and to confer toward the goal of the child recording that meaning accurately and well (even if it is only in the drawings). "So this is your family? Where is your mom?" I might say. Or, looking at the child's visual description of her mom, I might ask, "Where are her arms? No arms? She has to have arms, you silly, you know that!" I try to help children make their drawings more representational because I want to help children learn that "writing" involves conjuring up images of a subject and then recording whatever is in the writer's mind's eye onto the page. This is a basic premise behind all literacy. Learning to add detail to a drawing can be a precursor to learning to add detail to a written text. Learning to tell and draw what happened next (and to move from one page

to an extended story) can happen first around stories that are drawn and later around texts that are written.

It's crucial to convey from the start that stories need to make sense. I listen with great care to children's stories, making sure I can actually follow the child's meaning enough to say back a coherent story. If I find a child's story confusing, I let the child know this and recruit the child to rectify my confusion.

Children in this category may or may not have some print on the page. If there *are* letters there, I'll ask the child to read the message (even if I expect it can't be deciphered), and I will join in to help if the child has trouble. I won't give up easily on the job of discerning what has been said. The writer will see that I'm intent on deciphering what he or she has written. I focus through the errors to the content.

If the child *does* read his or her print to me, or otherwise acts as if the writing says *something*, I'll be glad. I know that some children write down letters simply to inventory the alphabet letters and the words they know and can produce. It is not unusual for a child who is in the early phases of learning written language to copy or list words rather than to write a message. Sometimes the copied letters mean the child has taken his or her very first step and is trying to assume the identity of being a writer, but other times the copied letters reflect a child's anxiety and lack of understanding that the letters only matter when they convey meaning. Either way, I redirect the child who has copied or made letters and words without an intention to convey meaning to think of something he or she has done and to draw that subject. Then I respond as I described in the incident when the child told me about watching cartoons and eating cereal in the morning. My goal will be to help this child learn that to write, you first must fill yourself up with content that is important to you and then reach for whatever means possible—drawing or writing—to convey that content.

If a child hasn't written at all, it is crucial to realize that this doesn't mean the child is hesitant or unable to write! Until we nudge the child a bit, it's impossible to draw any conclusions from an absence of print. And so I ask these children to tell me their story and then I say, "That is so cool! Why don't you write that?" I repeat the words the child said—perhaps the message was "I climbed the mountain"—and then I say with confidence, "Write that." I say this as if I don't dream my instruction to write could possibly cause a problem. I point as I speak to a blank space on the page and keep my eyes fixed expectantly on that portion of the page. If the child doesn't immediately turn his or her attention to writing, I often go so far as to dictate, "I . . ." and again I stare at and gesture toward the page as if certain the word I have just dictated will arrive there very soon. This moment is always a revealing one! If I keep my gaze fixed on the page and wait for the child to act, the child will follow my gaze and an extraordinary number of children will actually write. If a child says, "Is it *i*?" (or, conceivably, "Is it *e*?"), I avoid confirming the child's every guess. "Put down whatever you hear," I say with a confirming tone. When the child has written something—anything—I wait to see whether he or she will keep going. If the child seems stymied, I coach the child to reread what he or she has written (reproducing whatever the child intended to write whether or not that is, in fact, what is recorded on the page). I help in a way that brings forth the next word—*climbed*. Again, I direct my gaze *to the paper* and watch with bated breath.

The child in this instance may produce random strings of letters or letterlike shapes (see the next discussion). Alternatively, the child may spell words by recording the dominant sounds (correctly or not), or the child may appeal for help. The help I'm apt to give is described under the later heading "Some Children Benefit from Labeling Their Drawings." Whatever the child does when nudged to write will be instructive.

SOME CHILDREN WILL WRITE SQUIGGLES INSTEAD OF LETTERS

If a child uses diamonds, squiggles, approximated letters, or what appear to be random letters, it's tempting to think, "This child doesn't know the first thing about writing." If we look again, however, we can see that such a child may have mastered some essential concepts. These could include the writing concepts shown in the box on page 12.

If the child has only a shaky grasp of the idea that texts carry stories, or if the child's oral stories are underdeveloped, we may decide to focus for a few weeks on helping these children draw and tell stories that contain several pages of drawings, each accompanied by writing-like squiggles and by an oral text that is coherent and full of the child's emerging literary voice. This will support the child's sense of story and grasp on literary language. We will also find opportunities in the school day to teach this

Essential Writing Concepts

- Being able to make gross approximations of the fifty-two geometric forms that constitute the uppercase and lowercase English alphabet (practice is necessary to become proficient with these shapes).

- Knowing that writing involves recurring letters mixed together in ways that make words and that these letters are not reversible. An F is not the same as an ?.

- Knowing how to "read" writing (even if it's lollipops, not letters) with finger and eyes moving from left to right and top to bottom and—rather than snaking left to right, then on the next line, right to left—making a return sweep.

- Knowing that long utterances are represented by longer chunks of print and that when we read, we make oral utterances that accompany—and in some way match—the written marks.

- Knowing that pages in a book are usually not self-contained, but instead, one page combines with the next to create one coherent text.

child sound-letter correspondence so that his or her spellings during the writing workshop can soon become more conventional. After the child has spent a few weeks studying sound-letter correspondence at other times of the day—during phonics instruction, interactive writing, and shared reading—we'll move this child toward using sound-letter correspondences in order to label their drawings (this work is described below).

Other children who "write" with squiggles may already produce rich oral stories. These children will profit from being encouraged right away to label their drawings (also see below).

SOME CHILDREN BENEFIT FROM LABELING THEIR DRAWINGS

Although some children may enter school using lollipops, squiggles, and diamonds to represent oral language, once in school, all children will be immersed in work with alphabet letters. They'll study their own and other children's names and talk about the environmental labels in the classroom and in life: "What might this stop sign say? The first letter is *s*, like in Sam." Children will read alphabet books and make them too, featuring perhaps just the letters in a given child's name. They'll sort and categorize and make letters. Within three or four weeks of the opening of school, kindergarten children will have enough of an emerging knowledge of letters and sounds that we can teach them to label their drawings.

A word of caution! If emphasis on recording letters during the writing workshop isn't tied to a parallel emphasis on conveying content, some children will merely copy the alphabet chart or anything else they can find. One way to prevent this is to help a child approach writing by first remembering something that happened in the child's life, drawing that event over a sequence of pages, and only then writing the words that accompany the story.

In order for a child to record letters to represent a word, the child needs to listen closely to the sounds within the word. Children don't usually arrive in kindergarten knowing that *dog* (and *ship*) each contain three sounds (the technical word for these speech sounds is *phonemes*). Many five-year-olds who are asked to tap out the sounds in *cat* will hear the initial and final sounds only. When children write, they are learning to hear and distinguish sounds in words (this is *phonemic awareness*). Children need to not only hear a sound but also match that sound to a letter, recording it. "Let's say *me*," I say to the child. "Say it with me." Together we say /mmmeee/ slowly. "What sound do you hear at the start of *me*?" I ask. I may add, "Watch me, watch my mouth," and together the child and I again say /mmm/ and concentrate on the way our mouths feel as they make the sound. In this way, I help the child isolate the sound at the start of *me*, which is an important step. Now pressing on, I ask, "What letter makes /mmm/?" If the child suggests *any* letter, right or wrong, I ask the child to record that letter.

The child may have no idea what the letter could be, in

which case I will probably demonstrate how I think about this. Maybe I will repeat the /m/ sound and think to myself, "Have I seen *any* words that start with /m/—/m/—*me*, /m/—*Mom*, /m/—*McDonald's*." I may continue, "It's like /m/—*Mike*," and point to a nearby *m* in the name chart. After deciding the /m/ sound can be written by the letter *m*, I write an *m* and encourage the child to copy this letter onto his paper. "So let's read what you've written," I then say, recruiting the child to point under the letter and to read what he's written.

If the child required this much help with that first sound in the word *me*, I would not be apt to try for other letters within the word. The child will probably reread the one letter as if it says the entire word—*me*. Then I'll direct the child's attention to another part of the drawing and we'll repeat the process of labeling something else. Chances are good that again we'll record only the initial or dominant consonant. Soon I'll move to another child, leaving the first child with instructions to continue labeling the cat, brother, or sun. Soon children will begin to hear more than one sound in many words. I don't aim for correctness when children are labeling. Once labels report the dominant consonants in a word (*sn* for *sun*), I move the child toward writing stories that are carried by a one or two sentence caption under the drawing on each of several pages.

SOME CHILDREN WILL SOON WRITE SENTENCES

Just as it will be clear right away that some children will need support before they can even label, it will also be clear that with just a bit of encouragement and support, some children can soon write "I ride my bike" using letters to convey at least the initial or dominant sound in the words: *I rd mi bk*.

At first, we may be at the child's side to initiate and support this process. "What's happening in your picture?" I ask, and when the child answers, I say, "You need to write that!" Then I dictate the first word. "I. . . ." After the child has written, I help her regain the momentum needed to press on by helping her reread in such a way that she generates more text. "Okay, let's reread what you have written so far. 'I. . . .' Now what?"

Although this sort of scaffolding can be helpful and necessary at first, it is equally necessary for us to pull back some of our support so that the child is nudged to continue as best he or she can. Of course this will mean that the child bypasses a word or two, uses incorrect letters, and generally messes up. That's the price of independence. Our goal must be to withdraw our scaffold in such a way that the child continues voicing the next word, saying it slowly, and recording letters. We need to be ready to accept the child's approximations. If we jump in to be sure the child's approximations are correct, we keep the child in a dependent relationship to us, and the child will only write when we are on call.

Once a child has written one sentence, *we* often feel exhausted and our tendency is to signal, "Great, now you are done." It is wise to remember instead that if a child can write one sentence, he or she can write two sentences. If the child can write a few sentences on one page, the child can easily move on to a second page. . . .

SOME CHILDREN WRITE STORIES (AND A HOST OF OTHER GENRES, TOO!)

Depending on the grade level we teach, there will be, at the start of the year, some children who write sentences easily. Remember that every child deserves to start where he or she is as a writer *and to be challenged to go farther*. On the fourth day of first grade, Omid's folder showed three papers, each featuring a rather conventional drawing and fairly conventional text. One said, "I like school. We riyt at school. We reed at school." Meanwhile Omid had drawn a conventional picture of a butterfly, rainbow, and flower.

"What's your writing about?" I asked. Omid looked momentarily startled by the question but rose to the occasion and said in a stacatto sentence that sounded like dictation, "The—uh—the—whatjamacallit—the—butterfly—loves—the—flower."

"Tell me about you and butterflies," I said, trying to bring Omid toward content that mattered more to him.

"I never saw one," he answered. He was silent and I

Fig. 2-1 Omid

A moth was in my house. I got a box and threw it out of my house.
The box had oil in it. The moth was hurt a lot.
The moth fell down on the floor.
And that was the day that a moth was in my house.

waited, waited, waited. Brightening up, Omid said, "But I saw a moth! I was trying to get it out of my house. I took a box and I put it very close to it and I pushed it in and I let it go in the air." He gestured to show me how the adventure had gone.

"Omid," I responded, "you've got to write that!" Then I said, "It'll probably be a long story. You are going to need a few pages!" I stapled three pages together. Then touching the first, I asked, "What will go on this page?" Omid wasn't sure. "Can you remember how your story about finding the moth went?" I asked and looked up into the sky as if I were mentally reaching to re-create the event. Omid joined me and said, as if dictating the story, "A moth was in my house and. . . ."

"Okay, write that," I responded, pointing to the page. I dictated his words back to him, "A—moth—" Within fifteen minutes of writing, Omid had written the pages shown in Figure 2-1.

Although Omid had initially written lists of attributes ("Dinosaurs are big. Dinosaurs are nice. I love dinosaurs"), he had soon written a coherent story that spanned several pages. If a child is able to write a story, over time that child can learn to develop a setting, to show the internal as well as the external events, to write with literary language, to include dialogue, to decide which moments in the story are especially important and

to magnify those, and to incorporate techniques other writers have used. Children can not only write stories but can also write in a full range of genres for a full range of purposes. Attribute books can become information books with chapters elaborating on different aspects of a subject. There is no particular sequence to these developments, and most of them are within grasp for children at a surprisingly young age, as long as children are explicitly taught what they need to know, given opportunities for approximation with scaffolding, and encouraged to work toward greater independence.

Lucille Clifton, the great American poet, once said to a colleague and me, "It's important to nurture your image of what's possible. We can only create what we can imagine." It's crucial that we teachers nurture our image of what's possible for young writers. Figures 2-2 and 2-3 are pieces of writing written by first graders in the spring of the year. These represent the horizon we need to reach toward as teachers of young writers. As you read these pieces, guard against the very human tendency to dismiss them by saying, "Those children are gifted." These pieces are well written but are not beyond the reach of many first graders (let alone second graders!), assuming those children are gifted with the opportunity to study with teachers whose expectations are high.

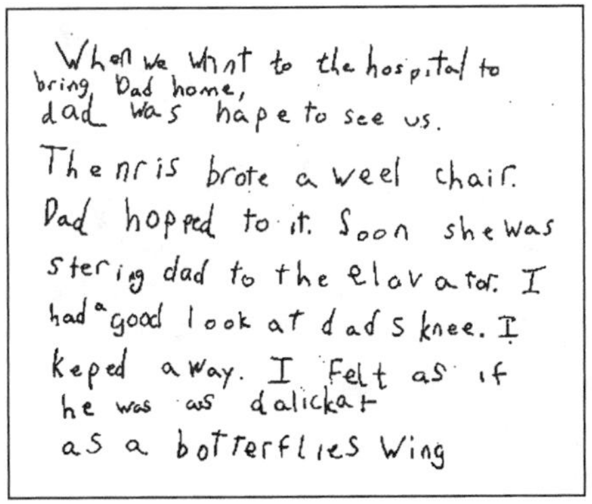
When we whnt to the hospital to
bring Dad home,
dad was hape to see us.
Thenris brote a weel chair.
Dad hopped to it. Soon shewas
stering dad to the elavator. I
had a good look at dads knee. I
keped away. I Felt as if
he was as dalickat
as a botterflies Wing

When we went to the hospital to
bring Dad home,
Dad was happy to see us.
The nurse brought a wheel chair.
Dad hopped to it. Soon she was
steering Dad to the elevator. I
had a good look at Dad's knee. I
kept away. I felt as if
he was as delicate
as a butterfly's wing.

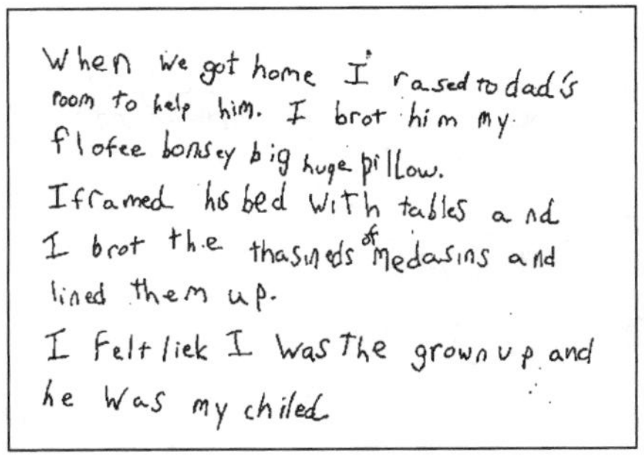
When we got home I rased to dad's
room to help him. I brot him my
flofee bonsey big huge pillow.
Iframed his bed with tables and
I brot the thasunds of medasins and
lined them up.
I Felt liek I was the grownup and
he was my chiled.

When we got home I raced to Dad's
room to help him. I brought him my
fluffy, bouncy, big huge pillow.
I framed his bed with tables and
I brought the thousands of medicines and
lined them up.
I felt like I was the grown up and
he was my child.

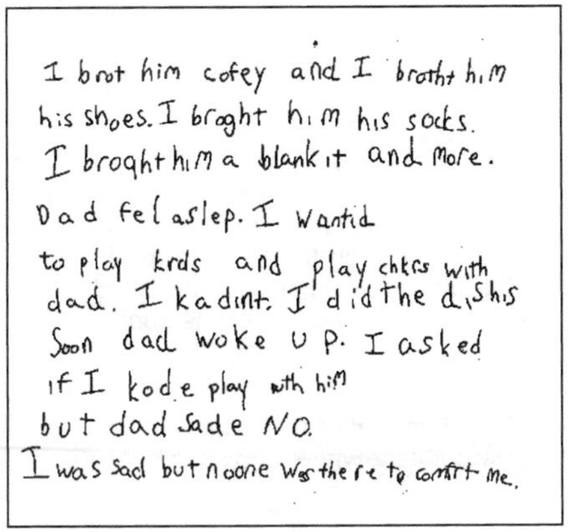
I brot him cofey and I brotht him
his shoes. I broght him his socks.
I broghthim a blankit and more.
Dad fel aslep. I wantid
to play krds and play chkrs with
dad. I kadint. I did the dishs
Soon dad woke up. I asked
if I kode play with him
but dad sade NO.
I was sad but noone was there to comfrt me.

I brought him coffee and I brought him
his shoes. I brought him his socks.
I brought him a blanket and more.
Dad fell asleep. I wanted
to play cards and play checkers with
dad. I couldn't. I did the dishes.
Soon Dad woke up. I asked
if I could play with him
but Dad said no.
I was sad but no one was there to
comfort me.

Fig. 2-2

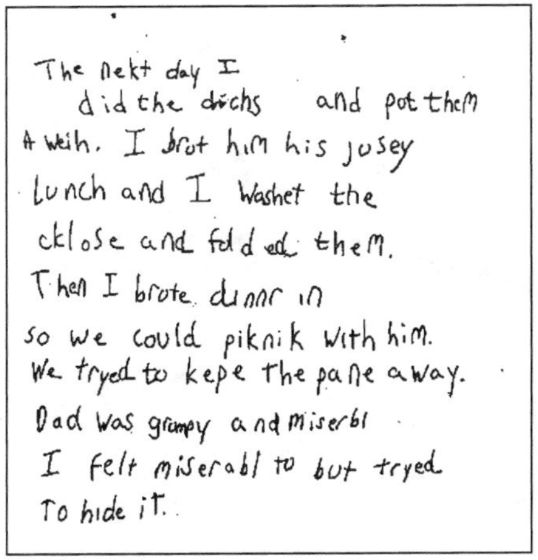
The next day I
did the dichs and pot them
A weih. I brot him his josey
lunch and I washet the
cklose and folded them.
Then I brote dinnr in
so we could piknik with him.
We tryed to kepe the pane away.
Dad was grumpy and miserbl
I felt miserabl to but tryed
To hide it.

The next day I
did the dishes again and put them
away. I brought him his juicy
lunch and I washed the
clothes and folded them.
Then I brought dinner in
so we could picnic with him.
We tried to keep the pain away.
Dad was grumpy and miserable.
I felt miserable but tried
to hide it.

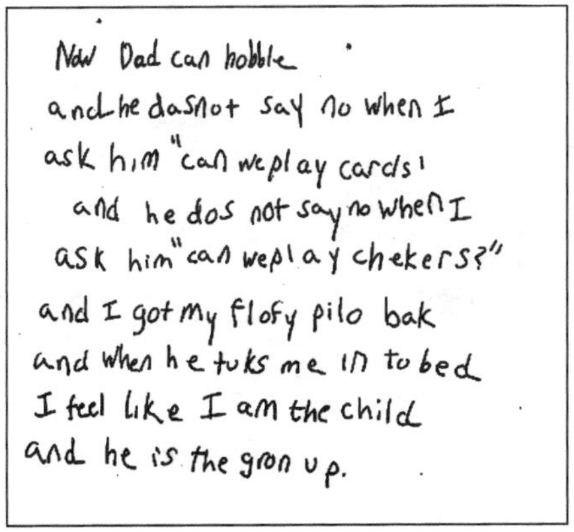
Now Dad can hobble
and he dasnot say no when I
ask him "can we play cards!
and he dos not say no when I
ask him "can weplay chekers?"
and I got my flofy pilo bak
and when he tuks me in to bed
I feel like I am the child
and he is the gron up.

Now Dad can hobble
and he doesn't say no when I
ask him, "Can we play cards?"
and he does not say no when I
ask, "Can we play checkers?"
and I got my fluffy pillow back
and when he tucks me in to bed
I feel like I am the child
and he is the grown up.

I was four years old. I took swimming lessons.

My teacher's name was Roberto.

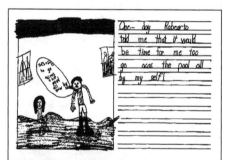

One day Roberto told me that it would be time for me to go across the pool all by myself!

"One, two, three," he said. I knew what that meant. It meant that I would have to go across the pool. I let go of the wall. But then I clutched the wall with a enormous amount of fear.

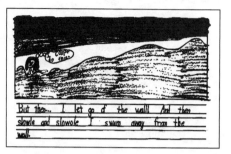

But then . . . I let go of the wall! And then slowly and slowly I swam away from the wall.

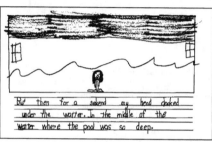

But then for a second my head dunked under the water. In the middle of the water where the pool was so deep.

I sank to the bottom of the pool.

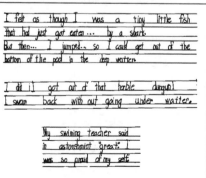

I felt as though I was a tiny little fish that had just gotten eaten . . . by a shark. But then . . . I jumped . . . so I could get out of the bottom of the pool in the deep water.

I did. I got out of that horrible dungeon! I swam back without going underwater.

My swimming teacher said in astonishment, "great." I was so proud of myself.

Fig. 2-3

PLANNING CURRICULUM IN A PRIMARY WRITING WORKSHOP

In the teaching of writing, curriculum comes from both the ongoing structures that last across the year and from the changing units of study that provide learners with their course to travel. The ongoing structures include minilessons, conferences, partnerships, writing folders, work time, and the like. Together, these structures provide the continuity of daily practice and coaching that allows learners to exercise and improve their skills. This is necessary whether the learner is a gymnast, a programmer, a mathematician, or a writer. The units of study, on the other hand, allow teachers to plan and organize a sequence of instruction so that over time students successfully tackle new and often increasingly difficult challenges.

Too many teachers provide *either* the ongoing structures *or* the changing units of study, but not both. Those who err on the side of providing only the ongoing structures tend to be child-centered in their approach to schooling, suggesting that children be allowed to write and that teachers watch from the sidelines, ever ready to seize teachable moments as they fly by. Those who err on the side of providing only the changing units of study tend, on the other hand, to be teacher-centered in their approach to schooling, suggesting that teachers should actively plan, compose, and carry out their teaching and that the children will join in if they can, in hopes that their teachers' hard work will rub off on them. What's necessary is education that requires high input from both children and their teachers. This rigorous balance is best achieved when curriculum involves *both* ongoing structures and changing units of study and when the curriculum provides the context for constant assessment-based instruction.

In the schools where I work closely, the teachers across each grade level in a school spend a day toward the end of the school year planning a shared curricular calendar for both reading and writing instruction throughout the upcoming year. These teachers use curricular calendars that the Teachers College Reading and Writing Project publishes as a starting place, revising our suggestions based on their own passions and knowledge and based also on the information they glean about their incoming children. The Teachers College Reading and Writing Project's recommended calendars are designed with New York State's rigorous assessments and the National Center for Education and Economy standards in mind, and teachers from other states sometimes need to alter the curriculum to take into account their state's standards and assessments.

If teachers across a grade level feel confined by the prospect of moving in synchronicity through shared curricular calendars, they designate particular months as times for divergent units of study; that is, perhaps everyone agrees to go separate ways in January and in May. The good news, then, is that for much of the year teachers can still benefit from being able to work together. When teachers across a grade level agree to travel in synchronicity, they are able to plan and reflect collaboratively.

Grade-level meetings can become a time for teachers to swap ideas for their minilessons, to wrestle with shared problems, and to function as a curricular support group. This structure also allows professional development to be aligned with instruction. A staff developer, for example, can work for a month in four schools, one day a week in each, then spend one day a week in a second cluster of schools, and return during the third month to the first schools. While the staff developer is working with a school, he or she helps groups of teachers at one or two grade levels plan and teach new units of study. Early on, the staff developer provides demonstration teaching and coaching to support that unit of study; over time, he or she provides coaching and guided practice as teachers assume more and more responsibility.

For example, a staff developer might work Wednesdays at P.S. 260, starting each day with an 8:30–9:30 "lab site" class of third graders, with all the second- and third-grade teachers participating. Later in the day, the staff developer might work similarly with all the kindergarten and first-grade teachers and then with all the fourth- and fifth-grade teachers. The staff developer would also need to lead a study group for each of the three groups of teachers, helping them plan their teaching for the upcoming week. As the unit of study nears an end and the staff developer prepares to leave to spend the next month with different schools, he or she helps the study groups plan for and perhaps launch the upcoming unit of study, which these groups of teachers will teach on their own. Perhaps when the staff developer returns, the teachers will collaborate and construct the unit of study so that now the staff developer can lead a parallel unit of study *for teachers* on a topic such as designing more assessment-based instruction or using small-group instruction across a unit of study. When teachers across a grade level share curricular calendars, it is easier to ensure that professional development directly supports classroom teaching.

Beginning on the next page, I will give an overview of and an explanation for the sequence of units we recommend across a year of K–2 writing instruction. Each of these units is described in detail in one of the books in this series, seven of which are being published in the original set and several others of which will come later. I will also overview the process and share the principles we draw on when planning *any* unit of study.

Dear Kindergarten Teacher,

I know there is a world of difference between kindergartners and first graders and that you will be tempted to surmise that these units weren't tailored for your little ones. I want you to know that my colleagues and I developed these units exactly for your very young children. We have taught these units to as many kindergarten children as first-grade children. I promise that if you trust enough to hang in there, the work your little ones do will astonish you and them and everyone who peeks into your classroom.

Meanwhile, your children will be the talk of the town and they will enter first grade with strengths no one dreamt were possible. In the schools I know best, this has happened again and again. Often these are schools brim-full of English language learners and children who didn't have the chance to attend nursery school, and yet for these children, as for others, the writing workshops transform our expectations.

You will notice that I do not tarry long before nudging children to write using conventional sound-letter correspondence. Let me explain my rationale. I also want to tell you about ways I alter the sequence in these units when I believe children need more time, which is sometimes the case.

First, here is my rationale for nudging children to begin writing with letters and sounds as soon as possible. One reason is that I have expectations for their writing. For example, the Primary Literacy Standards published by the National Center on Education and the Economy suggest that by the end of kindergarten, most kindergarten children should be able to write long texts—perhaps six pages long, with a sentence or two on each page. These texts should be fairly easy for you and I to read even though they aren't spelled conventionally. I helped to author those standards and they match what I see in classrooms where there is a daily writing workshop and teachers teach into that writing.

I also keep in mind that by January, most kindergarten teachers launch most of their children into reading little books (Levels A and B). I embrace the research by Elizabeth Sulzby and Marie Clay that suggests that before children are ready to profit from this sort of reading, they should be able to write with enough sound-letter correspondence that you and I can decipher much of what they write. Equally important, they should be able to reread much of their writing conventionally, matching what they say with what they have written in such a way that they notice and self-correct when the oral and written texts deviate.

But most of all, I encourage kindergartners to spell as best they can because I believe that when children need a knowledge of letters and sounds in order to write their own important stories, their investment in learning about print skyrockets. And so, even if a child doesn't know any sound-letter correspondences at all, I will encourage that child to find a picture he or she wants to label, say the word slowly, listen to the sounds in it, and then try writing the sounds onto the page. If the child is going around asking, "How do I write /ssss/?" I think this is the greatest possible context for teaching that child about the letter *s*.

For these reasons, then, I try to make sure that by the end of September every kindergarten child is writing his or her name on every story and is at least labeling items from the drawing. I hope each child will label by saying the word slowly, listening to the sounds, and trying to hear and record the first sound, then other sounds. I know that listening to and isolating sounds is phonemic awareness at it's best, and I expect kindergartners to do other work with phonemic awareness as well. I also expect that every day these children will learn something about sound-letter correspondence during a daily ten-minute interactive writing session (see the CD-ROM) and during shared reading. I will meanwhile teach children to hear and record more and more sounds in words and to rely on a handful of high-frequency words—Mom, I, me, and their own name.

The units we propose depend upon most children, by mid-October, being able to label *sun* as "sn" and *rabbit* as "rbt," in which case I graduate children to writing sentences under their pictures, leaving spaces between words.

My hope is that by mid-November, most of our children will be able to write a lot of text in such a way that at least you (and hopefully they) can read much of what they write. The time frame will be too ambitious for some kindergartners, and if this is the case, I suggest you add a detour study in October on Labels and Labeling books. I describe this briefly in my overview of the yearlong curriculum.

I hope this helps get you started off on the right foot!

Sincerely,
Lucy Calkins

A Recommended Curricular Calendar

Unit 1

Launching the Writing Workshop

In this unit, we help all children see themselves as authors. We ensure that each child can carry on during the writing workshop, choosing topics, planning for writing, and drafting as best as he or she can. It is essential that during this first unit of study, writers learn the rituals and structures of a writing workshop so they can carry on with some independence while their teacher moves about, conferring with individuals and small groups. The only way to be sure all children can carry on with independence in the first month of the school year is for us to lower our expectations for the actual writing students will do.

We begin the year by telling children they will all be authors. Then we help all children think up stories to tell, to draw, and perhaps to write. All children revise, if only by adding details into their pictures. Within a week or two, they revise also by drawing what happens next on a second page (which creates the very exciting chance to staple and literally grow books). Soon we point out that picture books have a place for drawings and a place for words, and we nudge every child to write words as best they can. (Some will have written words from the start, others will need our scaffolding.) We then use the Pathways (from Chapter 2) to inform us as we nudge writers from scribbles to random strings of letters, from random strings to labels, and from labels to stories.

Whether writers write just a few labels on items in their pictures or write paragraphs, by the end of this unit all children know that in order to write, a writer fills him or herself with an idea, plans how the text will go, and then draws and writes as best he or she can, working to make the page match the writer's vision.

Optional Unit

Labels and Label Books

This is an optional unit recommended for some kindergarten classes and for some classrooms filled with English language learners. The unit provides a way to help children focus both on the fact that writing represents the world and has real-world purposes and on the graphophonics involved in turning oral language into print. We launch the unit by saying, "Now that you are writers, I wonder if you'd help me fix up this room. We need to write labels on our meeting area and our library and our math area so people know what these places are for." The actual amount of writing required in a label is limited, so this gives children an opportunity to focus on recording sounds they hear in a word. Children first write functional signs for their classroom. They label the block area, perhaps labeling even the big blocks and the little ones. They might write a sign for the hamster's cage, or a sign saying "Please throw trash away" beside the trash can. These pieces are put to immediate use. The sign telling the hamster's name is prominently displayed beside the cage, the rules for using the trash can or the paints are prominently displayed.

Children are soon also labeling pictures in their own books. You may decide for a time to continue steering them to write (tell) about real events in their lives, labeling the objects in their pictures as they do so. Alternatively, you may shift to writing label books in which they name, page by page, the parts of something bigger. These books resemble many of the very earliest books children read. Now their books might proceed like one of these:

- *My Family:* Mom/Dad/Joline/Tiger/Me!
- *The Baseball Game:* the players/the fans/the ball/the game
- *A Firetruck:* wheels/ladder/hose/firemen/I love firetrucks.

In this way, students learn that writing serves a purpose and matches the picture, and they also receive intense help with sound-letter correspondence.

October (November)	**Unit 2** *Small Moments: Personal Narrative Writing*	We help children value tiny moments from their lives and know that writers hold these moments in their minds and hearts, then make a story out of them, one that stretches across a sequence of several pages. Instead of writing about the whole move from the old house to the new one, a child writes about saying good-bye to Annie. The story begins with the writer knocking on her friend's door, then the good-bye, then the writer's feelings as she walks away. We encourage writers to reread what they've written, to see details they may have overlooked or confusions they may have created or feelings they want to bring out. Writers revise as part of writing, easily and in an effort to tell the truth and to put life onto the page in ways that match reality and make sense.

This unit of study emphasizes certain qualities of good writing, including focus, detail, sequence, and writing with a sense of story. Alongside the emphasis on content and craft, there must be ongoing work on hearing and recording sounds, using known words, tackling words, leaving spaces between words, and being a risk taker with spelling.

November (December)	**Unit 3** *Writing for Readers: Teaching Skills and Strategies*	This study begins with us confessing to our children that we had a hard time reading their writing. Prior to now, we will have acted as if children's invented spellings are fine and dandy. We've reveled in their approximations. Now, we let the cat out of the bag. "I took your wonderful books home last night," we say, "And I sat down to read them. But do you know what? I read a bit and then I got stuck. I couldn't figure out what the story was supposed to say! Has that ever happened to any of you?"

Until now, we've so wanted our children to feel good as writers that we have hidden our struggles to translate their spindly letters into meaning. The problem with this is that the only reason children will care about spelling, punctuation, or white space is that these conventions make it easier for others to read and to appreciate their texts!

It's *crucial*, therefore, that as soon as a child can conceivably stretch himself or herself enough to be able to write in ways that others can read, we let kids in on the truth. If we're going to let kids in on the fact that sometimes we can't read the writing that we've until now accepted with such open arms, we need to do this in a way that doesn't cause children to despair. Our goal is to spotlight the importance of spelling and punctuation by designing a unit of study that makes word walls, blends, and capital letters into the talk of the town—and to do this while safeguarding children's focus on meaning and their love of writing.In this unit, the child first aims to write for the teacher, who tries mightily to read what children are writing and asks them to help by writing left to right and top to bottom, by including more sounds, by leaving spaces between words, and by incorporating word wall words into their texts. Children soon write also in hopes that *they* can reread their own writing. When writers are ready, we encourage them to write in a way that a partner can read their writing.

A commitment to revision is part and parcel of a commitment to teach writing as a process. Writing is a powerful tool for thinking precisely, because when we write, we can take fleeting memories, insights, and images and hold them in our hands. When we talk, our thoughts float away. When we write, we put our thoughts onto paper and can stick them in our pocket. We can come back to them later. We can reread our first thoughts and see that we have more to say. We can look again and see that our story has gaps or that our points are undeveloped. We can see that our sequence "jumps all over the place," or that our readers will think, "Huh?" Through rereading and revision, writing becomes a tool for thinking.

Watch a child at work making something—anything—and one sees revision. The child pats a ball of clay into a pancake to make a duck pond, and then revises the duck pond by creating a fingertip rainstorm that dapples the water surface. Young children revise block castles to add protected hiding spots for archers, and they revise pictures of spaceships to add explosions. They revise clay rabbits to make one ear droop. Young children can revise their writing with equal ease and enthusiasm—as long as we don't expect their revisions to look like those a grown-up would make. First graders can revise—as long as we expect their six-year-old best!

In this unit, children learn that revision is a compliment to good work. They select their best pieces from the fall and put these in a special revision folder and then revise one after another. They learn to use strategies (cutting, stapling, adding into the middle of a page, resequencing) in combination with goals (making sense, answering the reader's questions, showing not telling, adding detail, developing characters). The unit ends with children learning that they can revise writing also by thinking, "How else could I write this?" and then by turning their narratives into poems, stories, directions, or letters.

The most important message we give to children during a writing workshop is this: "You are writers, like writers the world over." It makes sense, then, that for at least one unit of study, children are invited to look closely at the work of one writer and let that writer function as a mentor.

When deciding on the whole-class mentor author, a teacher needs to decide if he or she wants this unit to continue the emphasis on writing personal narratives (or small moments) or to broaden the class's repertoire and launch other kinds of writing. Many teachers in our community decide to select an author who has written a few texts that are rather like the Small Moment stories the children have been writing, so that the author serves as a mentor in this work. But it is wonderful if the author writes other kinds of texts, too. The unit of study, then, can begin with studying an author's Small Moment stories and then move to studying other kinds of writing the author has written, opening the doors to the children, also, to create a whole range of kinds of writing.

We especially recommend K–2 children study Angela Johnson, Ezra Jack Keats, Joanne Ryder, or Donald Crews, although there are other wonderful possibilities. It is important to search for an author whose texts seem to children to be within their zone of proximal development.

In an author study, the class explores how this author lives as a writer, the themes the author tends to write about, but above all, the author's craft techniques. We first encourage children to look very closely at one text, pointing to sections they like and then asking, "What did the author do to create this nice part?" Soon children can also ask, "Did the author do that same thing anywhere else in this book? In another book?" Children find it thrilling to find three or four places in a text where an author uses the same craft technique differently, and these different instances in which one technique has been used help children see that they, too, can put the techniques into effect. Children tend to notice and emulate first the very concrete, obvious techniques, such as ellipses, but good teaching can help children realize that the ellipses creates dramatic tension (although we don't necessarily use that term!), which is a fundamental feature in effective stories.

After participating in a shared author study, each child is invited to choose his or her own mentor author, again noticing not only the author's writerly life and topic and genre choices but also her or his craft techniques. Students then develop their own writing projects, nourished by their own mentor author. The final portion of this study especially encourages independence.

February and March	**Unit 6**
	Nonfiction Writing: Procedures and Reports

This unit opens with us inviting children to become not only writers but also teachers and then suggesting that they use writing as a way to teach others. First, we help them teach others how to do something by inviting them to write books in which they draw and then tell a sequence of steps they hope their readers will take. Procedural writing requires explicitness, clarity, sequence. This is a genre that requires writers to write with an especially keen attention to their audience, anticipating what their readers will need to know and when they'll need to know it.

Then the unit shifts so that for the remaining few weeks each child writes just one, very long All-About book on a topic of his or her choice. The experience of writing these books will introduce children to the format of information books and lead them toward report writing, but we think it is best for children to write in this genre first around topics in which they have personal experience (soccer, baby brothers). Some teachers bring children through this unit twice, with the second cycle supporting each child writing on one instance of a whole-class theme (for example, each writes on one insect).

When children write non-narrative texts, we need to teach them to impose an organizational structure on their "pile of stuff." These books are written in chapters, with children sorting information by means of tables of contents. If a child is writing "All About Dogs" and one page is on "Training Your Dog to Heel," we teach the child to use paper formatted to support procedural texts. Other pages will be formatted differently to support other ways of organizing informational writing. Teachers also teach children to notice and emulate a few text features of nonfiction writing (diagrams, charts, a table of contents, sub-headings, etc.).

April (May)	**Unit 7**
	Poetry: Powerful Thoughts in Tiny Packages

In the poetry genre study, children practice and consolidate all they've learned so far, and do so while working with more independence. They find significance in the ordinary details of their lives, draft pieces that are filled with specific detail, employ revision strategies in the service of qualities of good writing, emulate techniques other authors demonstrate, and edit their work so that others can read and enjoy it.

Meanwhile, much of our instruction is designed to help children explore and savor language. We encourage them to live as poets, seeing the world with fresh eyes and reaching for the precisely honest and carefully chosen word. We stress that poets write for the ear and listen to the music in their words. We help children realize that language can create images and that there's a world of difference between *fry* and *sizzle*, *shine* and *sparkle*, *cry* and *weep*. We also try to find child-appropriate ways to introduce children to figurative language, knowing that some of them use metaphor and simile naturally and could benefit from using them deliberately as well.

Optional Unit

Fiction

The urge to write fiction begins when children are very young. Allowing children to satisfy this urge taps an energy source that is something to behold. In this unit, we help children tell and plan stories, perhaps "across their fingers" or as they turn five or six pages in a book. We help students internalize the rhythm and structure of stories and anticipate how stories tend to go. "Usually your story has a character who feels something and tries for something, but then there's trouble and the character has to work, to try, to struggle," we say. And then we let students draft a bunch of stories, selecting their best to revise.

Optional Unit

Writing for Many Purposes

In this unit, we remind children of all the kinds of writing that exists in the classroom, the school, and their homes. "You can write in all these ways!" we say, issuing a grand invitation for them to write for a variety of purposes, including recipes, invitations, pamphlets, songs, book reviews, etc. We add new varieties of paper to accentuate the new possibilities and hope that the writing projects children do in school spill over into their homes. The emphasis is on learning how genres look and sound and on writing all day long, across our whole lives, for real purposes. ("Look at what you read in your life and let it inspire you to write in similar ways.")

Children in this unit may begin to keep a class mailbox, to write a real magazine that is published for the whole school, or to take on a service project that involves real-world functional writing.

This unit comes at the end of a yearlong study of writing and it reminds children that they can be the authors of their own writing lives. The year ends with us saying to children, "You all are writers—go to it!" and then encouraging youngsters to imagine and pursue writing projects of their own.

Principles that Inform the Plans for Every Unit of Study in the Primary Writing Workshop

Plan for children to write a lot.

Within any unit of study in a primary writing workshop, children work on a lot of pieces of writing. A unit on how-to writing, therefore, doesn't culminate in the production of a single how-to book. Instead, children generally write at least two texts a week. At the end of a unit, children may be asked to select just one text to perfect for publication, but they will have written many more texts. During the unit on revision (and conceivably other units), children revise previously written pieces rather than generating new pieces.

Plan for the entire unit, with all its parts.

When we plan a unit of study, it helps to think of the unit as a journey with bends in the road. Although we can't imagine each of the small steps in the journey, we approach the journey with a general plan for the bends in the road. We can describe our plan for a unit by saying, "First we'll spend a few days on . . . , then we'll . . . , after that we'll. . . ." In a sense, a unit of study is like a story, and we need to approach any unit with a clear plan for at least its beginning, middle, and end.

Plan what we'll do for each part of the unit and what children will do.

When planning a unit of study, it is helpful to think about what children will probably be doing as writers as they travel along any one bend in the road and also to think about what we will probably be teaching during any one bend in the road. These two things will not always be exactly aligned. In a spring unit on poetry, for example, children will do a lot of work they have learned to do from other units. They'll choose topics, draft and revise poems, scissor apart texts, add details. Meanwhile, we may focus instruction on a few new aspects of the work—the importance of patterns, for example, or of figurative language.

Plan for continuity–in texts, metaphors, and language.

Before a unit begins, it's helpful to anticipate the threads of coherence that will run through the unit. For example, you will want to think about whether there will be a shared metaphor in your unit so that you don't talk one day about the ingredients of a poem, the next day about the importance of growing poems, and the next day about the lens for looking at poems. If you can stay with one way of talking about your subject, children are more apt to internalize the language and concepts you teach. Think also about whether you'll want to revisit a single text often during a unit. If so, what will you attend to in that text early in the unit, later on, and later still? Will your children be able to read this text? How will they—and you—mine it for its teaching potential? In many units, the text that travels across the unit and gives it coherence will be a text you (or you and the class) write. This text will probably begin as a very brief text and it will probably be about an experience the class shared.

Plan to support ongoing writing goals as well as unit-specific goals.

We approach each unit with a set of goals, but there are also many goals that endure across all units. Over time, it is important for writers to learn to plan for what they'll write, to write in ways that are increasingly conventional, then to reread and revise their writing. Eventually it is also important for writers to study exemplar texts and try out techniques other authors have used. Writers of any age can learn to cycle through all these stages of the writing process without a teacher prompting them along. Plan to instruct children in the use of a new writing tool in every unit.

Plan to instruct children in the use of a new writing tool in every unit.

Each new unit of study can be embodied in a new tool. During a unit on "Can you read this?" children will be given personal copies of the word wall. During a unit on revision, children work with scissors, tape, and a revision pen. During an author study unit, children begin to use a seed-idea booklet and a chart in which they name techniques they see other authors use. Each of these tools remains with writers after the unit is over as a visual reminder that the units are meant to make lasting impressions.

Plan to end the unit with a celebration.

Each unit ends with a few days to "fix up and fancy up" the work children have done, culminating in an authors' celebration. These celebrations are done differently for different units, but in general, across the year they become more elaborate.

Plan to SAVE some of every child's writing and to start new pieces or kinds of writing with every unit.

After a unit ends with a celebration, some of the work is sent home, save for selected pieces that are transferred to children's cumulative portfolios. Sometimes you'll decide to keep children's writing because you plan to have children revisit it in an upcoming unit of study. (Keep the work from the fall until the revision unit is completed.) Either way, however, children enter a new unit of study with a cleaned-out writing folder, planning to write new pieces or planning new work with selected former pieces.

CHAPTER 4

MANAGING THE WRITING WORKSHOP

Managing children so they carry on as writers and so they work with independence and rigor is a very big deal. When we plan our writing instruction, we must plan not only the words out of our mouths—the minilessons and the conferences that will convey content about good writing—but also the structures and systems that can allow us to manage a crew of young writers.

Why do so many people assume that it is only *novice* teachers who struggle with classroom management? Why do people talk about *classroom* management as if it were on a level with doing the laundry? Why is classroom management regarded as a low-level skill when *corporate* management is considered an executive skill? If the people working under our direction were grown-ups instead of children, the job of managing the workers would be regarded as highly demanding leadership work. Executives take courses on designing accountability structures and structuring workspaces and on holding workers accountable. As classroom teachers, we also need to give careful attention to these issues.

I tell teachers to assume from the start that classroom management will be a challenge and to give careful thought to instituting systems that allow children to work. How could it *not* be tricky to build an environment in which twenty or thirty youngsters each invent and pursue his or her own important projects as writers, working within the confines of a small room, each needing his or her own mix of silence and collaboration, time and deadline, resources and one another? The good news is that none of us must invent management systems ex nihilo.

The Importance of Structures and Systems

I recently visited the classroom of a first-year teacher. The writing workshop was about to begin. "Writers," Alexi said, "Let's gather." As if on cue, Alexi's twenty-eight children gathered on the carpet, each sitting on top of a decorated writing folder, shoulder to shoulder with a longterm writing partner. Alexi took her place in "the author's chair," and began leading a ten-minute minilesson in which she named a strategy that writers often use that she wanted to teach, then demonstrated that strategy, gave her children a few minutes of guided practice with the strategy, and invited her writers to add that strategy to their repertoire. Soon Alexi's children had dispersed to their writing spots, each hard at work on his or her own ongoing writing project. As I watched all this, I marveled that Alexi, a novice teacher, was teaching in such efficient and effective ways. Had someone

sprinkled Miracle-Gro on her? I remembered with a pang my first years as a teacher. "How did she get to be so good?" I wondered, but then I knew. Alexi is the teacher she is because although she is new to the profession, her methods are not new. Her methods have gone through hundreds of drafts, and have been shaped by the legacy of scores of experienced teachers.

When teachers study together, it's not just novice teachers whose teaching stands on the shoulders of others. This is true for us all. It is no small achievement to establish the structures and expectations that ensure that all our children will work with engagement and tenacity at their own important writing projects. Unless children can sustain work with some independence, teachers will not be free to teach. How important it is, then, for teachers to compile what we know on this important topic.

In 1986, when I wrote the first edition of the now classic *The Art of Teaching Writing*, I emphasized the importance of keeping workshops simple and predictable. Over all these years, this injunction continues to be an important one. Back then, I wrote:

> *If the writing workshop is always changing, always haphazard, children remain pawns waiting for their teacher's agenda. For this reason and others, I think it is important for each day's workshop to have a clear, simple structure. Children should know what to expect. This allows them to carry on; it frees the teacher from choreographing activities and allows time for listening.* How *we structure the workshop is less important than* that *we structure it. (pp. 25–26)*

> *I used to think that in order to teach creative writing I needed to have a creative management system. I thought creative environments, by definition, were ever changing, complex, and stimulating. Every day my classroom was*

different: one day we wrote for ten minutes, another day, not at all; sometimes students exchanged papers, and other days they turned them in; sometimes they published their writing, sometimes they didn't. My classroom was a whirlwind, a kaleidoscope, and I felt very creative. Rightly so. My days were full of planning, scheming, experimenting, replanning. Meanwhile my children waited on my changing agendas. They could not develop their own rhythms and strategies because they were controlled by mine. They could not plan, because they never knew what tomorrow would hold. They could only wait.

I have finally realized that the most creative environments in our society are not the kaleidoscopic environments in which everything is always changing and complex. They are, instead, the predictable and consistent ones: the scholar's library, the researcher's laboratory, the artist's studio. Each of these environments is deliberately kept predictable and simple because the work at hand and the changing interactions around that work are so unpredictable and complex. (p. 12)

LEARNING ABOUT STRUCTURES AND SYSTEMS

The best way I know to learn classroom management strategies is to visit several well-established writing workshops while paying special attention to the infrastructure that underlies this kind of teaching. Writing workshops are structured in such predictable, consistent ways that the infrastructure of any one workshop remains almost the same throughout the year and throughout a child's elementary school experience. This means that when we visit a writing workshop, we peek in on not only today's but also tomorrow's teaching. In this chapter, we'll visit a few primary-level writing workshops when they're in full swing, and we'll pay special attention to the nitty-gritty of classroom management. I'll be at your side on this tour, commenting on what we see together. We'll pay special attention to these lasting structures:

The Environment for Writing Instruction
- Room Arrangements
- Materials
- Schedule

Managing Each Component of the Writing Workshop
- Managing the Mianilesson: The Beginning of Each Day's Writing Instruction
- Managing Writing Time: The Heart and Soul of the Writing Workshop
  - Sending Children Off to Work: The Transition from Minilesson to Work Time
  - The Nature of Children's Work During the Writing Workshop
  - Conversations in the Writing Workshop: Friendships, Partnerships, and Silent Writing Time
- Managing the Share Session: Workshop Closure

When There Are Management Troubles

The Environment for Writing Instruction

Teaching writing does not require elaborate materials or special classroom arrangements. Teachers who teach in widely divergent ways can all set aside time for the teaching of writing and can offer children direct instruction in good writing. There are, however, a few room arrangements that especially support the teaching of writing, and teachers may want to consider arranging their classrooms around the shared principles described in this section.

ROOM ARRANGEMENTS As we walk along the corridor peeking into classrooms, you will see that in most of these classrooms, one corner has been filled with a nine-by-twelve carpet framed on several sides with bookcases, creating a library area that doubles as a meeting space. These carpets (and the communities we create as we gather on them) are important enough that when I recently met with a long-time Project principal after he'd been promoted to the position of a New York City superintendent, he greeted me by saying, "Lucy, you'll be glad to know we put carpets into one thousand classrooms already." Usually, one corner of this carpet features a large chair referred to as "the author's chair," in honor of the times children sit there to read their work aloud (although actually the teacher sits in this chair the most), with teaching equipment nearby, including an easel with chart paper, markers, and a fine-tipped pointer. If possible, teachers keep an overhead projector nearby with a ready wall on which to project enlarged texts.

Although the meeting space is important in these classrooms, the most important thing is the rhythm of children sometimes pulling close around the teacher for a short stretch of very clear, explicit instruction, followed by children dispersing to their work places, with the teacher now meeting with individuals and sometimes small groups as children write. In many of these classrooms, children do this work at tables or else at desks that have been clustered together to form small tablelike seating arrangements. Sometimes teachers tell us they do not have space enough for a carpeted meeting area and for children to work at clusters of desks or at tables. Although this may sound strange to you, in more than a few classrooms, teachers create more space by foregoing some of their chairs. They can only do this if they unscrew the bottom half of the legs on (or otherwise lower) a table or two. Using tables low enough so that children can sit around them without chairs creates space in an otherwise crowded classroom and allows children to sit in different ways at different times of the day. The low tables are often set in a carpeted area alongside the carpeted library corner, and children who work at these tables kneel or sit on their bottoms. In some classrooms, table lamps on these tables (and in the library) create a soft glow.

MATERIALS When writing is an important part of a teacher's literacy curriculum, it is crucial for the teacher to develop a system for managing children's actual papers. In most writing classrooms, teachers find it helpful to give each child a writing folder, and to color-dot the folders so children who sit at the blue table, for example, have a blue box for their blue-dotted folders. When it is time for the writing workshop to begin, a table monitor brings the box of the appropriate-color-dotted folders to the appropriate-color table. Each child is taught to remove the piece he or she has been working on from his or her folder and then, in order to keep the workplace clear, to return the folder to its box, which is kept nearby for easy access.

All the child's recent work is kept in the folder. It is crucial that work is dated each day with that day's date stamp. This makes it very easy for a teacher to look through a child's folder and re-create what the child did in the writing workshop on Monday, Tuesday, Wednesday, and so on. Principals often sit down with writing folders as part of their supervision and want to see evidence of children's ongoing work. In many classrooms, children have a red dot on the left pocket inside their folders for finished (stopped) work and a green dot on the right pocket for continuing ("go," or in-progress) work. While children work in a particular unit—poetry, say—they write and revise many texts that pertain to that unit. Early in the year children write two or three pieces a week. As the year progresses, they tend to write fewer but longer pieces and to spend more time revising and editing a piece.

When units of study end (at approximately one-month intervals throughout the year), each child selects one piece to improve and "fancy up" for publication. Publication always involves an authors' celebration, usually on the final day of a unit of study. These tend to become more elaborate as the school year progresses. The first authors' celebration might be as simple as parading around the room carrying finished pieces of writing that are then fastened to a "We Are Authors" bulletin board. Then the bulletin board might be toasted with juice and celebrated with cookies. Later in the year, a more elaborate authors' celebration might turn the classroom into a "museum" with children's work displayed on desks and with visitors invited to roam among the displays. During these celebrations, we would never ask the entire class to listen as each and every child reads a piece of writing aloud. If published work can be word-processed by an adult, then a copy or two of each child's published piece becomes an important part of the class library, available for readers. When this happens, children will often read their own and one another's writing during the reading workshop.

At the end of a unit, the pieces that are not published in any fancy way get divided up. Some are mailed or given to particular readers. At least one original piece is saved in the child's cumulative portfolio. The remaining stash of work is usually sent home in a take-home folder (although there are times, including the first few months of the year, when the work is saved in school instead). The particular system I describe here isn't essential. What *is* essential is that each child in the school needs to date each day's work, that children's work needs to accumulate until the authors' celebration, and that any system of clearing out the folders by sending work home can't start until teachers have an opportunity to talk to parents about the hard work and significant progress that are evident in their children's spelling. This usually means we keep work in school until Open School night, teacher-parent conferences, or until the first grade-by-grade parent meetings. By then, explanations about children's spellings will be accompanied by convincing evidence of growth, and it will not be hard to reassure parents that incomplete spellings are a sign not of lax but of high standards.

On the counter alongside the folders, there are toolboxes for writing tools, with as many toolboxes as there are tables (or other writing work areas). At the start of writing time, a table monitor from each table sets that table's toolbox at the center of the table. By December, the toolboxes contain scissors, Scotch tape, a date stamp, and a variety of writing implements, including pens, pencils, and perhaps markers. Most teachers keep a can of newly sharpened pencils in each toolbox and ask children to avoid sharpening pencils during the writing workshop. Instead, the entire set of pencils is sharpened as part of morning jobs. If a child breaks a pencil point, the child simply puts the broken pencil in the "to be sharpened" can. If children write with pencils, we ask them not to use erasers. (We tell children we want to see and admire their drafts and revisions.) The community usually owns these pencils and other tools, so that any child can draw from the collection as needed. Because tools are less expensive when bulk-ordered, most teachers ask parents to contribute toward the cost of school supplies, and the teachers order these supplies in bulk. Some supplies that are ordered at the start of the year are withheld until they are needed.

Many teachers supply children with thin marker pens rather than pencils. The supply of marker pens often runs low a few months into the year, just when children are less apt to need this incentive to draw and write. Pens or pencils do fine as replacements, and the transition from one set of tools to another can support the transition from coloring toward sketching, from spending a lot of time on the picture toward a greater focus on the writing.

In most of the classrooms I know best, there are one or two "writing centers" in the classroom, each containing a variety of paper for children to use as they need. That is, the term *writing center* describes a place where writing supplies are stored and distributed, not a small-group activity that takes place while a teacher leads small reading groups! Children do not sit in the writing center to write. Instead, they go to the writing center to secure supplies. Teachers tend to offer only a few paper choices at the start of the year; as the year progresses, they expand the number of options.

The design of primary writing paper matters tremendously because the materials convey expectations. The important thing is for teachers to assess their writers and to help children make paper choices that provide the right balance of support and challenge. Over the course of a school year, the paper on which children write needs to change so that children are nudged toward writing with the expected stamina and volume! (Templates for these pieces of paper can be found on the CD-ROM.)

The yearlong progress of paper for one kindergarten child might go as follows:

A first grader may progress along this sequence of paper:

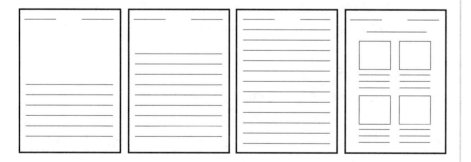

The system for dispersing paper and utensils is not crucial. What *is* crucial is that children need to be able to independently access their ongoing texts and obtain more paper without a teacher spending time on this. The system for dealing with materials needs to be streamlined enough that it doesn't require more than a few minutes of a teacher's attention each day.

For reasons that will become more clear over the course of this book, I do not recommend that young children write in spiral notebooks, journals, or diaries. This may surprise readers who are familiar with my ideas for upper elementary and middle-school children. "Don't you encourage children to keep writers' notebooks?" you may ask, and the answer is that yes, starting in third grade I encourage children to keep writers' notebooks. But there is a vast difference between the writers' notebooks some children in upper-grade classrooms keep and the journals I so often see in primary classrooms. Too often, these journals are containers for writing that has no genre and no audience (other than perhaps the teacher) and that is never revised, edited, or published. Because I want children to understand why people write and to draft and revise writing for readers, I vastly prefer inviting children to write all the kinds of writing they see in the world. As part and parcel of this, I encourage children to write on a variety of paper, but especially in small booklets that are easily revised.

On the walls of these classrooms, charts and shared texts serve as references. Usually classrooms contain an alphabetically organized word wall on which about forty high frequency words are displayed (far fewer in kindergarten or at the start of any year), often held in place with Velcro. In some classrooms, particular words on the word wall bear a star; these are words (such as *at*) that can beget zillions of other words. Most of the classrooms also display an enlarged list of children's names, and in kindergarten and first grade these lists are studied extensively, especially at the start of the year as part of phonics instruction. There are also lists containing words organized by sound (as in perhaps a list of ō words). There are always several charts that support children's writing. In one room we visit, one chart lists qualities of good writing and another chart lists revision strategies.

SCHEDULE Time is the most precious resource we have, and each teacher will need to design his or her schedule so that it is aligned to state, district, and school standards and expectations, as well as to the teacher's values and the children's development levels and needs. The schedule will be somewhat different in kindergarten and first grade than in second grade, with children in kindergarten and first grade receiving more time for dramatic play and blocks. Here are two possible daily schedules in which a teacher may devote two and a half hours a day to reading and writing instruction (as many will).

   If other things must be squeezed into a day, another option is to cycle one component out of each day, so that writing, choice, thematic studies, math, and the special each occur four rather than five times a week.

Managing Each Component of the Writing Workshop

MANAGING THE MINILESSON: THE BEGINNING OF EACH DAY'S WRITING INSTRUCTION The writing workshop starts with a signal for writers to set their supplies out on their tables and to gather for a minilesson. It helps to have a consistent way

Schedule 1

Prior to 8:30	Unpack, jobs, sign in, talk
8:30 – 8:45	Morning Meeting (songs, picture book or poems, shared reading of the daily schedule, phonemic awareness, alphabet work with names, etc.)
8:45 – 9:45	Writing Workshop (ten-minute minilesson, forty-minute work time punctuated by five-minute mid-workshop advice, and ten-minute share)
9:45 – 10:15	Choice (dramatic play, blocks, alphabet center, art)
10:15 – 10:45	Phonics (including shared reading and interactive writing)
10:45 – 11:45	Reading Workshop (minilesson that includes shared reading or a read-aloud; private reading; partner reading or centers—conferring, guided reading, and strategy lessons occur simultaneously)
11:45 – 12:30	Lunch & recess
12:30 – 1:00	Thematic studies (may include interactive writing, shared reading, or reading aloud)
1:00 – 1:40	Special (dance, drama, science, art)
1:40 – 2:30	Math (includes calendar work some people do not do at start of day)
2:30 – 3:00	Read-aloud and book talk

Schedule 2

Prior to 8:30	Unpack, jobs, sign in, talk
8:30 – 8:40	Morning Meeting (as above)
8:40 – 9:40	Reading Workshop (as above)
9:40 – 10:40	Choice/Thematic Study
10:40 – 11:40	Writing Workshop (as above)
11:40 – 12:10	Phonics (as above)
12:10 – 12:50	Lunch & recess
12:50 – 1:40	Math
1:40 – 2:20	Special (dance, drama, science, art)
2:20 – 3:00	Read-aloud and book talk

to signal for children's attention. It also helps to use this same signal whether we want to ask children to gather for a writing minilesson or for a math lesson. One teacher sends a messenger to move among children saying, "Five minutes until writing time." Others sing out, "Stop, look, and listen," and wait for children to freeze, look at them, and sing back in a lovely echo, "Oh, yeah." In the quietness after this exchange, these teachers say, "Writers, let's gather," or give some other instruction.

Rather than trying to give new detailed instructions each day itemizing what children will need to bring to that day's minilesson, most teachers find it efficient to ask children to always bring their writing folders (which generally contain a pencil or pen, slid into the pocket). If children sit on their folders, this keeps the materials out of the way of fiddling fingers, yet accessible when they are needed. Kindergartners, however, are less apt to refer to their drafts during a minilesson, and so they often keep their folders in their writing spots, each child taking out the text he or she will work on that day and only *then* convening in the meeting area. The fact that these children have already laid out their writing tightens the transition between a minilesson and writing time and increases the likelihood that the minilesson carries over to children's work.

When they gather on the carpet, children usually sit in assigned spots beside an assigned, long-term partner. Because children in our classrooms also have reading partners and those partners need to be able to read the same books (which consequently means they are ability-matched), we make a special point of establishing writing partnerships that bring together children who are quite different from each other. We regard a partnership as peers who help each other, however, *not* as one teacher partner and one student partner. Partnerships last at least the length of a unit of study, if not longer. When particular partnerships work well, we try to keep them in place over time. It's a great thing in life to find someone who can help us with our writing. If children are English language learners, the partnerships often contain a more and a less proficient speaker of English. For new arrivals, the partnerships may be language-based, two speakers of Urdu working together, for example.

During the minilesson, we teach children a strategy they can use often as they write. These strategies are multilevel, pertaining to all writers, and are ones that can be used again and again during the writing workshop and during children's lives as writers. We lead minilessons about the strategies spellers and writers use, about the characteristics of a genre and the qualities of good writing, and about the norms and practices of the writing workshop. Chapter 5 in this book is devoted to the subject of minilessons, and the accompanying books in the series each contain approximately fifteen minilessons and suggestions for dozens more.

Often a teacher will pause in the midst of a minilesson and ask children to try what the teacher has just taught. Primary-level children can't organize themselves to do a quick burst of writing on the spot, and so for this age level the active involvement phase of a minilesson usually means children turn to their partner and try something aloud. For example, if a teacher demonstrates how she uses precise words to describe something exactly—a plant, say—she may then say, "So turn to your partner. Partner one, try to use exact words to say what you notice when you look closely at partner two's shoe." Teachers teach children how to switch from listening to the teacher to interacting with a partner. Sometimes, for example, teachers ask children to sit with legs crossed "like a pretzel" and then, when they turn to their assigned partner, to sit "knee to knee."

Often minilessons are extensions of each other. First-grade teacher Pat Bleichman, for example, recently taught a "string of minilessons" on the importance of pausing to reread one's writing. In the first minilesson, she role-played the writer who makes the momentous decision to reread and rework what she's already written (now displayed on the easel) rather than moving on to a new piece. While rereading, this writer noticed details that were missing from her drawing and added those. Then she reread, her finger pointing under the words, and saw that, "Oh no!" she had omitted a word. Pat used a carat to insert the missing word. During the next day's minilesson, Pat again supported the central message that writers often reread and rethink finished work. This time, when Pat reread her story she realized that she had ideas that would require large-scale additions, and consequently she used not only a carat but a new sheet of paper to make space for revision.

MANAGING WRITING TIME: THE HEART AND SOUL OF THE WRITING WORKSHOP *Sending Children Off to Work: The Transition from Minilesson to Work Time* Minilessons end with the words, "Off you go," and we try to make it likely that children *do* "go off" and get started working. We teach children that writing time is precious and that it's important that they do not waste one precious moment of it. Sometimes we disperse

children in clusters. While one cluster goes off to work, we say to those that are still sitting near us on the carpet, "Let's watch and see if they *zoom* to their writing spots and get started right away!" If we speak in a stage whisper ("Oh, look, Joy has her paper out and her folder put neatly away! She's rereading what she wrote yesterday! How smart!"), the dispersing youngsters will hear us discussing them and they'll respond in all the expected ways.

Sometimes we disperse children by saying, "If you are going to be doing [one kind of work] today, get going." Then we say, "If you are going to be doing [another kind of writing work] today, get going." Finally we may say, "If you are not sure *what* to do today and need some help, stay here and I'll work with you," and soon we're leading a small group of children who've identified themselves as needing more direction.

It is easy to lose a tremendous amount of time in transitions, and therefore we need to teach children how to get started on their writing. It helps if children always know where they'll sit during writing time. In most classes, children have assigned writing spots. It can also help for children to know that the first thing writers do is to write their name on their papers (if this is a new paper and their name therefore isn't already there). If the child is adding to an already existing text, it can help to always begin by looking back and trying to reread yesterday's work. Once children are writing readable writing, these two tasks are fairly easy for writers to do. These two tasks, therefore, draw children toward more demanding work.

Many teachers find it helpful to convey to children that at the very start of any day's writing workshop, we are not immediately available for individual writing conferences. Too often, children leave the minilesson, arrive at their writing spots, and then sit passively until we cycle to the table, giving each child a personal "get started" nudge. This means that a lot of a child's work time ends up being consumed with waiting! If we notice that at the end of a minilesson half a dozen children swarm about looking for more explicit instructions, while others sit passively at their writing spots, we must resist the temptation to give an individualized version of the minilesson to each of the needy children.

Instead, we'll want to make it more likely that children hear and follow the instructions as we give them to the whole class. Have a paraprofessional or a student teacher sit among the children during the minilesson and ask this grown-up to model intense listening, drawing children into this sort of behavior. When we say, "Today, I want thus and so," this adult needs to elbow the child, signaling, "Listen up." We may want to create an interval for children to retell our directions to partners, talking across their fingers as they progress through the steps. Just after the minilesson, the adult may ask the child who never seems to comprehend and recall directions to confirm (say back) what the child heard. "Good listening today," the adult can say.

Some teachers regularly start the writing workshop by spending a few minutes watching children make the transition into writing. Instead of immediately hunkering down with one child, and then another, these teachers watch all children for a few minutes. As we watch, we may smooth out an issue or mobilize a few children who need just a nudge, but the most important thing we do is to make our quiet presence known with a touch, a word, a smile, a glance. We meanwhile research signs of trouble, so that later that day or another day we can address the real issues at the root of these problems. In these ways, we avoid the syndrome of starting each day's writing time by rushing among kids giving each one a personalized recap of the minilesson. If even after all this, a cluster of children wait passively for us to draw close, instead of giving each a private review of the minilesson and a personal nudge to begin, we will probably cluster the slow starters into a group, work with them, and then reiterate the charge, "Get started."

The Nature of Children's Work During the Writing Workshop   After children disperse to assigned writing nooks, they either resume their ongoing work on a piece or they begin a new piece. Every day, children draw and write as best they can, on topics of their own choice. Children always choose a topic, plan the piece, write it, revise it, put it in the finished-work section of their folders, and begin a new piece. The nature of the child's work will be determined by the unit—in one unit, children will be writing poems, in another they will be revising completed pieces from earlier in the year. In almost no instance will the teacher have determined the topic. That is, the minilesson is not the forum for assigning *what* children will be writing about that day. The subject is almost always chosen by the writer. Instead of assigning topics, the teacher teaches a skill or concept for the writer to keep in mind and to use as needed. A child's work is influenced by the day's minilesson, but children do not rely on the minilesson as the source of their work. One way to think of the role of a minilesson is to imagine a building principal calling his or her teachers together and reminding them of the importance of making wall charts that accompany their teaching. This principal would then say to the teachers, "Off you go," and they would head to their classrooms to continue the teaching they'd planned. They'd carry with them the reminder that it is wise to find opportunities in their teaching to make wall charts. In this instance the principal, like the teacher of a writing workshop, would hope that the instruction given will at the right moment raise the level of the ongoing work, but the principal certainly doesn't expect that the teachers will return to their classrooms and forego all plans to immediately spend a day on charts!

In Pat Bleichman's first grade, on the day she taught children to use carats to insert missing information, one child was writing a true story about finding an inchworm on her sock, another was writing a letter to the tooth fairy asking for five dollars, please, for a tooth that really hurt, and yet another writer was instructing kids in how to fix a squeaky skateboard. Each of these writers was expected to reread his or her writing to make sure it made sense, using carats to insert missing words, but they were also expected to do many things they'd learned from other days' minilessons. For example, it was not an accident that in this class, writers had chosen not only their topic but also their genre, nor was it an accident that they had chosen paper that matched their intentions. The letter to the tooth fairy was written on stationery in the form of a letter. The true story of the inchworm was written on pages that had been stapled together to make a book, and the instructions for fixing a skateboard were written on paper that had been folded like a brochure and contained boxed-in areas for drawings and diagrams. It was because of previous strings of minilessons that these children (who, on that day, were all making a special point to reread their writing) were

writing in a variety of genres for a variety of real-world purposes and selecting paper to match their images of what they wanted to make. Children produce work that represents every developmental level. (I worry when I *don't* see this.) One child will use fairly conventional spelling. Another child will represent the sounds she hears, which tend to be the initial and final consonants. All children are expected to incorporate the sounds, chunks of sounds, and sight words they know into their writing. Over time, children demonstrate a growing control over phonics, sight words, and the conventions of written language. (I discuss their sequence of development in Chapter 2.)

Conversations in the Writing Workshop: Friendships, Partnerships, and Silent Writing Time   While young children write, they talk companionably with each other. Most of the teachers I know best like young writers to work at tables rather than desks because this encourages the conversations that are vital to children's work. As young children work side by side, they make running commentaries. These commentaries do a lot to make writing workshops into the richest sort of language workshop imaginable. An adult who sits close to a table full of writers will hear talk like this:

> "My mom *feeds* baby mice. They are soooo cute!"
> "How do you spell *ee* like in happ*y*?"
> "Uncle, uncle, uncle, that's my uncle. Aunt, aunt. . . ."
> "Wait a minute. I got two *ms*."
> "Know what my puppy does? She bites her tail!"
> "Mine bites *me*!"
> "Help! My *y* is banging my *a* on the head. Oops! Look out!"

Of course, when we encourage children to work companionably alongside one another, talking quietly as they work, this can spiral into an environment in which no one gets any work done at all. Teachers need ways to signal to children that they are too loud. Many teachers use the same signal to quiet their classes that they use to pull their children together onto the carpet. "First graders," Amanda Hartman tends to say, in a surprisingly dominant yet quiet voice. Amanda's children know this is a signal that they *must* stop talking immediately *and look at her*. At the start of the year when she is instituting this procedure, Amanda will wait a very long time until everyone *is* silent and is looking right at her. Then she may simply put her finger to her mouth, and simply say, "Could you work more quietly please."

"I find that after I first teach this signal to children, I really need to use it a lot so they practice taking it seriously. For a week, I may use it two or three times in a writing workshop, and of course I'll use the same signal throughout the day," Amanda says. "It's always about consistency and follow-through. I can't be sporadic in my expectations that they'll quiet down and look at me." Amanda and others emphasize the importance of children's focusing on them visually because visual cueing-in fosters mental cueing-in. Once teachers have quieted the class, we may make some suggestions encouraging children to talk like writers or emphasizing the importance of using "two-inch" or "workshop" voices.

At some point midway through the year, some first-grade teachers decide that their children are mature enough to benefit from silent writing time, punctuated with deliberately chosen intervals for talk. These teachers tend to institute whole-class "private writing times" and whole-class intervals for partnership talk. Partnerships will exist long before a teacher suggests this division between silent writing times and partnership sharing times. As I described earlier, children sit beside their partners during minilessons and are often asked to turn and talk to their partner for a moment or two. Once children are accustomed to these scaffolded opportunities for talk, it is then a small step to have children meet in these same partnerships at the end of a writing workshop. Once the class is accustomed to having partnership interactions at the beginning and end of writing workshops, it's then a simple step to add a partner sharing time in the middle of a writing workshop. "Writers, can you gather in your rug spots," the teacher may say halfway through a writing workshop, and then set children up to work with their partners. "It can help to tell someone the story you are writing. Right now, will partner two tell partner one your story? Tell it with details— the whole thing—and tell it in a way that gives your partner goosebumps."

In some rooms, these mid-workshop partnership shares become an expected structure. In these classrooms, the partner shares help children stay on task. Children work for as long as the class can sustain a focus (which tends to be between twenty and thirty minutes). When the room grows restless, the teacher interrupts children's writing to say quietly, "Writers, please meet with your writing partners." Some days, the teacher steers these five-minute intervals so the partnership conversations reinforce that day's minilesson; other days these conversations instead counterbalance the minilesson. When Pat gave her minilesson on rereading and using carats to insert missing words, her instructions during this interval were, "Today, will partner two read your writing to partner one? Partner two, remember to point under the words with your

The Management That Makes One-to-One Conferences Possible

Keep moving so conferences can be short and frequent.

When we confer, we usually find it works best to move among children, conferring with them at their work places, dotting the room with our presence. Although we don't come close to reaching every child every day, we can hold individual conferences with four or five children a day (four or five minutes per conference), and this allows us to work with at least one child from every section of the room. If we sense that many children need more attention, we can make our presence matter more if, when talking with one child, we encourage nearby children to listen in. We deliberately ignore these listeners, looking intently into the face of the one child. This often spurs the listeners to eavesdrop all the more intently. Often, as our conference ends, we generalize it to the others who've listened in. "Do any of the rest of you want to try that too?" I ask. "Great! Do it! I can't wait to see."

Teach children never to interrupt when you are conferring.

We teach children that when we confer, we don't expect other children to interrupt the conference. Another child can come close and listen in, but he or she must wait until we've finished conferring to ask a question. If a child interrupts while we are conferring, we react in astonishment saying, "Don't you see that I'm conferring?"

Occasionally, share with the whole class the teaching in one conference.

During most workshops, after a few conferences, we ask for the whole class to look up, and we then make a teaching point. Once in a while, we address classroom management, but often this teaching point allows us to broadcast the insight one child gleaned from a conference. "Writers, can I tell you what Joannie and I just realized," we say and proceed to retell the events of one conference in ways that make it applicable to many children. Transcripts of these interventions are included in the units of study.

Create systems of dealing with daily occurrences that don't require your intervention.

We create bottlenecks if we tell children (or inadvertently convey to children) that they *must* come to us for bathroom passes, permission to get more paper, help spelling unknown words, support in using the stapler, permission to declare their piece finished, etc. If we notice a reliance on us, we need to reflect on how we inadvertently created that reliance and think, also, whether it is necessary. We can avoid bottlenecks and circumvent a number of problems by teaching kids wise ways of handling tricky spots in the writing workshop. We can, for example, lead minilessons on using a stapler, what to do when you're done, what writers do when they're stuck on a topic, and so forth.

Teach children how to solve predictable problems on their own.

When children come to us hoping for solutions to problems they could have resolved on their own, we try to remember that although it may be *easy* to simply *solve* the problem, we are wiser to take the time to put ourselves out of this job. "What do *you* think?" we ask. "So why don't you do that—and next time, I think you could solve a problem like this on your own." Alternatively, we might say, "I'm wondering if you need to come to me. I bet you can figure this out on your own."

Create a place where children who need a conference can go for your help.

If a child in the midst of writing decides that he or she needs help, we generally prefer that the child come to us (waiting until we finish conferring) rather than stay in his or her seat. Waiting in his or her seat, the child tends to be disruptive because he or she is stymied.

Concentrate on teaching the writing process, not on making every child's piece the best it can be.

Children need to be able to go through the entire process and begin another piece of writing without our necessarily intervening. For this to happen, we need to accept that they will do work that's less than perfect. We won't always be there to raise the level of their work and that's okay. All we can hope is that they will do their five- or six-year-old best. Over time, our teaching will lift the level of what kids do easily and on their own. In the meantime, if we're hyperinvested in every piece of work being as good as it can be, we're in for a lot of management trouble.

Create the expectation of a lot of writing work getting done each workshop time.

If children are expected to work hard and are held accountable for getting a lot done, the room will be more apt to have that wonderful "workshop hum." It is advisable, then, for teachers to think about how we can hold children accountable for getting a lot of work done during a writing workshop. If children don't get their math done during math time, they need to do it another time. Similarly, during writing time, there needs to be no option but to get a lot of writing done. If children aren't able to accomplish much work during class, we need to find other times for them to get the work done. The message needs to be clear that there is no option but to work hard.

Use strategy lessons when many children need the same conference.

Often we pull a small group of writers together who might benefit from the same sort of help. "I pulled you together," we might say, "because all of you seemed like you were having trouble getting started." We call this small-group instruction a strategy lesson, and we design strategy lessons so they resemble minilessons.

finger. Work together to make sure you can *both* read the text *and* be sure it makes sense. Fix it if you can. Use the carat if you need it. Then you can both get back to work." On that day, only partner two shared his or her writing. The teaching partner, partner one, knew that another day, roles would change and he or she would have a turn to receive help.

After these partner shares, the class continues to write for perhaps another fifteen minutes. Once again, the teacher circulates among children, holding writing conferences.

At some point during the workshop, the teacher usually brings four writers together for a small-group strategy lesson. One day, for example, the strategy lesson might be designed to spur writers to write with more details. "I called you together because I read your writing and I'm dying to learn more from each one of you! You didn't tell me any details. Rhonda, you said 'My cousins and I played,' but you didn't tell me *what* you played. Leo, you said, 'I love when my Nana comes,' but you didn't say what you do together." In some classrooms, after the teacher convenes a strategy lesson, the writers may be asked to sit at a special table for several days and help each other with whatever the teacher taught (which, in this instance, would be the project of adding more details into their true stories).

MANAGING THE SHARE SESSION: WORKSHOP CLOSURE The workshop ends with a share session, in which the class may convene on the rug again or may return to their partnership conversations. Either way, the teacher has a teaching point to make in the share, and she makes it while also helping children reflect on how one aspect of their work went. Children may hear the story of a child who tried a strategy the teacher recommended in that day's minilesson. "Nicole reread and, lo and behold, she, too, found that she had left something out and look at what she did! By golly, Nicole used a carat to fix her story!" The share often highlights one or two children's work in ways that illustrate and *extend* the minilesson. For example, if the minilesson was on using a carat, the teacher might celebrate a writer who not only used a carat but who also crossed out (!) a confusing section of his story. In an instance like this, the share provides an opportunity for what almost amounts to a second, minor-level minilesson. Sometimes the share session functions less as an extension of the minilesson and more as a support for the literate culture of the classroom. For example, this will be the occasion for children to hear about a classmate who got a response in the mail from an author or to learn about a child whose mother encloses notes in her lunch box. Sometimes the share begins as a time to talk about how it felt to try some new writing work. "How was it, noticing what your author did and trying to do the same?" a teacher might ask, and children could talk in a group or with their partners about whatever they'd experienced.

When There Are Management Troubles

When children don't carry on productively in a writing workshop, it's important to take the time to diagnose the cause, realizing that sometimes what appears as a classroom management problem is really an instructional problem. Sometimes, for example, a teacher and I may realize that the issue is not management but inspiration. That is, it could be that we need to make greater efforts to convince children that writing is worth doing by creating an environment in which writing and writers are cherished. Is there so much responsiveness to writing—to children's writing and to that of published authors—that children *want* to put their stories onto the page and share them? Then, too, sometimes trouble that appears at first to be a management-related issue in fact grows out of the fact that children feel stymied, overwhelmed, and anxious. It is important to check that the expectations we convey (even inadvertently) are multilevel enough that every child feels as if he or she has work to do that is within that child's grasp. Do *all* children feel that they can do work their teachers will honor? If children think that the writing their teachers value is beyond their reach, they will whine, delay, and line up for assistance—and this will create bottlenecks because there will not be enough help to go around. In the end, if children don't regard writing as doable and worth doing, they will either act out or tune out.

But often, if children aren't carrying on productively within the writing workshop, the problem falls solidly within the province of classroom management. Usually in these classrooms, teachers are so busy rushing from one child to the next that they don't have time to stop and study the patterns in their classrooms. How easy it is for me to sympathize with these teachers, because often I, too, am so busy running, running, running that I do not stop to ask, "Where am I going?" What each of us needs to remember is that the answer can't lie in our running faster and faster. There's got to be a better way, but we can only discover that way if we give ourselves time to observe, to think, and to secure help.

The first step requires that we become observers of our own classrooms. "Let's call kids to the meeting area and watch what it is that 95% of them do when they are asked to gather for a minilesson. Let's see what they do with automaticity, without us saying anything," I say to teachers, recruiting them to join me as observers. "Let's watch also what they *don't* do." Later we watch again at the transition point between the meeting and work time. During the workshop, too, we watch for the trouble spots. What happens if we don't rescue matters? Is it after a certain length of time that things become frayed—or in a certain section of the room? For certain individuals?

Teachers of very young children, especially, often believe that the particular set of management problems they face are inevitable, that these issues are part and parcel of the terrain of early childhood education. Some teachers believe that long lines of needy children, constant interruptions, and only brief stretches of time on task are par for the course in the primary grades. This mindset is a self-fulfilling prophecy. In these instances, the most helpful thing I can do is to take teachers with me to other classrooms filled with children who are like their own, and to ask them to join me in the margins of those rooms. I wish I could do that with you, my reader. I wish you and I could literally *time* the number of minutes it takes between the end of the minilesson and that lovely moment when a hush falls over the room and everyone is engaged. I'd want you to see that this transition needn't take more than three or four minutes. I'd want you to notice that many primary teachers *are* able to move among their children, that it is not pie in the sky to say that teachers hold five or six conferences a day. I'd want you to see that in many classrooms—yes, even in many of our crowded urban classrooms filled with learners who could be classified as at-risk—a teacher can confer for the whole workshop without a single child interrupting to say, "Can I. . . ." I'd want you to see that classrooms containing twenty-eight kindergartners can sustain the actual writing part of a writing workshop for at least forty minutes with only a single teacher cycling among them.

Sometimes when there are management troubles in a room, I wonder if perhaps no one helped the teacher anticipate that these problems would inevitably occur and therefore to plan how to respond to them. We needn't wait for the inevitable problem to arise before we devise a solution to it. In the real time of our teaching, the challenges happen very fast and we definitely don't have time to make considered responses. But in the mental movie of our anticipated teaching, we can stop action and think, "What will I say when a child interrupts the minilesson to tell me about a broken pencil?"

Early this year, I watched a first-grade teacher gather her children on the carpet and begin to read aloud Bill Martin's quietly suspenseful story *The Ghost-Eye Tree*. The room was hushed save for the teacher's voice and the voice of the story, which combined to cast a spell over the listeners, drawing us in. Then, out of nowhere, big-eyed sweet Mario stuck his hand up. Holding his pencil toward his teacher, he said, "Look, it broke." The teacher, clearly unsettled by the interruption, whispered, "You can go sharpen it." Then, as the kids made a path for Mario (who nevertheless stepped on two or three hands), the teacher valiantly tried to resume reading.

Watching this generous and kind teacher, I knew she was in for trouble. I knew the next time she gathered her children for a read-aloud or for a minilesson, there'd be many more children whose pencil broke, who got a little blood under a fingernail, who had a stone inside a shoe. The problem is, Mario's interruption of the read-aloud isn't a one-time-only event. This moment will be repeated over and over, all day, every day. If we rehearse for our teaching to go wrong (as it will), we can be ready to respond to the inevitable curve balls.

In the end, then, although we must teach writing in responsive and child-centered ways, our ability to teach writing relies on our willingness to plan, to assess, and to give respectful attention to the job of classroom management. Children learn to write from the work they do; therefore, establishing and managing a productive work environment is a critical aspect of good teaching.

TEACHING METHODS: MINILESSONS THAT POWER YOUR CURRICULUM

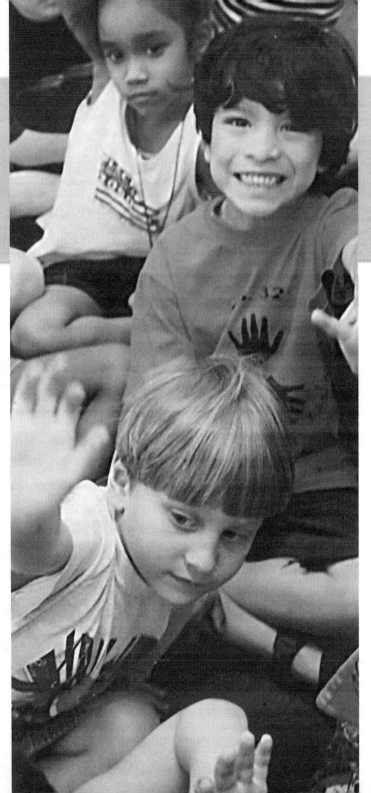

Just as the art instructor pulls students together to learn a new glaze or a new way to mix paints, just as the football coach huddles his team to go over a new play, so, too, the teacher of writing pulls children together for minilessons that generally start each day's writing workshop.

Minilessons, then, power our curriculum. Once we learn how to lead strong, efficient minilessons, we find we have a power chip that never quits. It generates strong teaching each day, each year. The teachers I teach often worry most over how they'll generate the *content* for their minilessons, and this will be the focus for much of this series. I'm convinced, however, that it's even more important for teachers to learn the *methods* of leading efficient, effective minilessons. When teachers study the craft of effective minilessons, this work can change our teaching not only in the writing workshop but also in every discipline, and it can improve not only our whole-class but also our small-group instruction.

Connection

Our minilessons begin with a *connection*. This is the "listen up" phase of a minilesson, and it generally lasts no longer than a minute. During the connection, we put today's minilesson into the context of the class's ongoing work. Often the connection begins with a sentence or two in which we recapitulate yesterday's work, followed by a precise example that illustrates the generality. "Yesterday we worked on. . . . You remember how Mario. . . ." We end the connection by telling children what we will teach them today that we hope they will carry with them not just today but into the future. For example, we might say, "Today, I will teach you that whenever you want to revise your writing, it helps to . . ." or "Today I will show you that when writers want to create good leads for their stories, it can help to. . . ." By the end of the connection we've "come out with it" and explicitly named exactly what we'll teach.

Teach

Next we teach students something we hope they'll use often as they write. We usually begin the teaching component by putting the strategy or concept we recommend into the larger context of either our writing or a child's writing. For example, if I want to teach students the characteristics of a strong lead to a story, I might say, "When I go to write a new story, I take up my pen and for a second, I pause and think, 'What shall I write?' Then I come up with a topic. But then I don't just start writing! Instead, I think, 'What would make a good beginning, a good lead?'" Alternately, I might retell the story of a child (or of lots of children) at work as writers. "Yesterday I noticed many of you getting started on your writing. You'd think and think about what to write about (braiding your sister's hair, falling off your bike) but as soon as you got your topic—presto! You were writing. That was weird to see, because after I get my topic, I always think, '*How* can I start my story?'" In one of these two ways, then, we often show children how and when they'll use the strategy we're about to teach. Then we name the strategy again. It is important to choose with care the words we use when we talk about writing, in hopes that they'll be memorable. After naming again the strategy or concept we'll teach, we start teaching it. To do so, we use one of four methods. We are most apt to *demonstrate* for children. Sometimes, instead, we *explain and show an example*. We occasionally involve the class in a tiny bit of *shared inquiry*. Sometimes we help the class learn by taking them through a bit of *guided practice*, although this is more apt to come during the next phase of the minilesson. Whichever method we use, we try to teach in a way that will connect with our students and make a lasting impression. Doing all this in four or five minutes is a tall order!

Active Engagement

After we teach something, we give children the opportunity to try what we've taught. Usually we do this by involving them in a bit of guided practice in which they do what we've taught while we interject lean, efficient prompts that either scaffold them through the steps of what we want them to do or lift the level of what they are doing. Sometimes it's not easy to create a brief "try it"; instead, children talk about what they've just seen us demonstrate. On those occasions, we usually ask them to tell a partner what they saw us—or someone else—do or to tell the partner what they plan to do next. No matter which method we use for this active involvement phase, children usually turn to talk with a partner. They may talk about what they saw us do, talk about their plans for that day, or talk through how they might do something we recommend writers do.

Link

We *link* the minilesson to the ongoing work of today's workshop. Sometimes the subject of the minilesson will only be pertinent for some writers that day. "How many of you will do this today?" we might ask. Other times, we want to be sure every writer incorporates the new strategy into his or her work that day. "Get started doing that right here on the rug," we might say. "Once you are started, you can get up and go to your writing spot." In these or other ways, we make it likely that at least some children transfer the minilesson to today's independent work, and we do what we can to remind children that today's minilesson has been designed to add to the repertoire of tools and strategies they bring to *every* day's writing.

Mid-Workshop Teaching Point

Often, halfway into the work time, we speak to the entire group. We may relay an observation from our conferences, highlight a particular example of good work, or steer children around a peer problem. Sometimes we suggest that children pull together with their writing partners to talk briefly about a subject we raise.

After the Workshop Share

At the end of the workshop (after writing time) we gather students in a share session in which we *follow up* on the minilesson. The share sessions have a teaching point, and they function almost as a separate and smaller minilesson.

The Architecture of Effective Minilessons

Our most effective minilessons tend to follow a similar structure. That is, while the *content* of the minilesson changes from day to day, the *architecture* of minilessons remains the same.

Putting the Pieces Together: One Minilesson

Abby Oxenhorn recently gathered her kindergartners on the carpet for a minilesson. "In reading for the last few days, we've been talking about how letter chunks can help us read tricky words," she began. "Well, today, we're going to talk about how letter chunks can help us also *as writers*!" This was the connection phase of her minilesson. Then Abby brought out a list of chunks with which the class was familiar. "So, we have a list of chunks that you all, as readers, know well," she said. As she pointed to each chunk, the children chimed in, reading in unison:

sh	*ing*
ch	*en*
th	*ook*
ph	

"And we also know words that make other words," Abby said, setting a second chart on the easel beside the first. Again the class read the list in unison:

all	*ill*
and	*in*
at	*it*

Now Abby said, "I'm going to do my writing now, and I want you to watch as I write my words. Notice how the chunks help me." This was Abby's preface to her demonstration.

Speaking almost as an aside, Abby said, "Yesterday I listened to you talk about gymnastics and remembered my gymnastics class. I'm so excited to start my story." Taking hold of a marker pen, she began voicing the words as she quickly wrote, "I loved gymnastics. The. . . ." Now she paused in her writing, looked up at the ceiling, and said "thing," to herself as if she wasn't quite sure how to spell it. "Th-ing" she said again, this time gesturing to the chart of chunks. "Wait a minute! Th-ing. Two letter chunks!" and she quickly wrote the word. Abby, of course, has no trouble spelling *thing*, but she was role-playing what she wanted her children to do and thinking aloud to show them her mind working.

After rereading her text, Abby continued voicing what she wanted to say and then writing it. This time she reread, then added on, saying (and writing), "The thing I loved most was . . ." and again she paused and slowly said, "handstands." She muttered (as if to herself), "That's a really tricky word. Let me see if these chunks can help. Hmmm," and she scanned her chart. She paused as if this was hard and looked over the chart again, all the while saying "handstands" to herself. By now most of the class had joined into the effort and were also searching the chart for chunks that could help with *handstands*. A flurry of children's hands went up. Turning to the class Abby said, "Whisper to your partner if you see *any way* those chunks could help me with *handstands*, but *don't tell me!*"

Abby continued her work. "H-and," she said, stretching the word out. Then, as we watched, it was as if the component chunks of the word dawned on her. "H-and! Look at that! H-and. There's an *and* inside *hand*."

This marked the end of the teaching phase, although in fact the active involvement stage had already begun. "Now what about *stands*?" Abby continued, having set the writers up for success. "Work with your partner and see if you can help me." Soon a child had helped Abby write this word using two chunks. After a bit, Abby told her class, "I'm going to say 'My mom sat.' I know *my* and *mom* but hmmm—*sat*? What do you think, partners? Help each other." Now it was again time for the kids to give it a go.

Finally Abby linked the minilesson to the writers' ongoing work. "Writers, will you give me a thumbs up if you think you'll use the idea of letter chunks when you are writing today!" The class responded as expected, and Abby assured her children that she'd be coming around to admire their chunks. "Put checks in the margins when you use a chunk so I can find them easily, because I'm going to be so excited to see this," she said.

THE ROLES WRITERS PLAY DURING A MINILESSON

We find it's helpful to teach children what *their* jobs will be in a minilesson. Explicitly. On more than one occasion, we'll say, "Today and every day in the minilesson, when I say, 'Writers, let's gather,' you'll get your writing folder and hurry here. You'll sit on your folders and you'll sit on your rug spot with your writing partner beside you. Then I'll talk to you for a few minutes. When I talk to you, you're going to really turn your brains onto high [we act this out] and *listen*, because I'm going to show you strategies you'll want to use in your writing. You'll do a lot of listening during that first part of the minilesson, and not a lot of talking." This introduces children to the connection and the teaching part of a minilesson. We also want children to understand the third component, active involvement, and so we also say, "Then after we show you something we hope will be helpful to you, you'll have time to try the strategy yourself, right here on the rug. Usually you'll turn to your partner and do some work together. Sometimes you'll be helping to think about a story the whole class is writing together. Then after the minilesson we'll go off to our writing spots, and you'll carry the strategies with you and use them as you write your own pieces on topics you choose." Our little speech doesn't mean children truly understand what is expected of them during minilessons. We need to teach in consistent ways, reminding children of our expectations.

The Components of a Minilesson

Connection

> We put today's work into the context of children's ongoing work and explicitly name what we will teach today. Whatever we teach will, we hope, be something children will use often as they write.

Notice that although the connection phase of Abby's minilesson lasted only a minute, there were still two sections to it. Abby began, as we almost always do, by picking up a thread from yesterday's work so that today's minilesson builds on prior work. The day after her lesson on writing with chunks, Abby could, for example, launch the next minilesson by saying, "Yesterday we learned that writers use letter chunks to help them write tricky words like *handstands*." Then she would move to the second part of her connection and tell children what she planned to teach them today. "Today I want to remind you that these chunks help us not only when we *write* but also when we *reread* our writing." That would then be the end of the connection phase.

Teachers could also begin the connection (that is, state the first half of the connection) by saying:

Last night I looked at your writing and I noticed quite a few of you were. . . . (And so today I want to show you. . . .)

or

Yesterday we learned that writers reread their writing to make sure it makes sense. (Today I want to tell you one more reason why writers reread their writing. Writers also reread their writing to appreciate the sounds of their writing.)

or

Many of you are writing true stories just like Miriam Cohen does. (Today I want us to look at how she starts her stories off and I want you to notice how her stories often begin with a character in the midst of action.)

One predictable problem we encounter during this phase is that some teachers have been taught that it is better to elicit information from children rather than to say anything to them in a straightforward way. The result is that some teachers begin the minilesson with a barrage of questions. "Class, yesterday we talked about what?" the teacher will ask. "And we were having trouble with what?" she'll add. Alternatively, the teacher might use questions to draw from children whatever it is she wants to say. "Today, class, I'm going to talk about the beginnings of your pieces. What are these called, class? It starts with an *l*. Is it called a *lead?* Today we're going to talk about writing strong leads."

Try to avoid launching minilessons with questions, and above all, avoid asking known-answer questions in which you're looking for a particular answer. Children can't read your mind, so their answers will take you off in different directions, turning a minilesson into a conversational swamp. When teachers use this occasion to barrage children with questions, kids learn to expect minilessons to be convoluted and circuitous. Why not, instead, realize you have the floor and try to speak in interesting and clear ways?

Then, too, sometimes teachers take this opportunity not only to refer to but to repeat yesterday's lesson. If this happens, we end up without enough time to be sure *today's* minilesson makes a lasting difference!

The final and most worrisome issue I see in the connecting phase of minilessons is that often teachers tell children what they'll be *doing* today, rather than telling them what they will *learn*. In a minilesson, my hope is that instead of saying, "Today we'll read and revise our poems," you will say, "Today, I will teach you the way a poet reads poetry, and you'll see that poets read their poems aloud, listening to the way their words sound."

Teaching

> We teach students a new tool or concept that we hope they will use often as they write.

Just because minilessons are brief, this doesn't mean they are effortless to plan. In fact, a rule of thumb is that teachers probably need to spend as much time planning a minilesson as we spend teaching it. Most of our time is spent planning the teaching and active engagement components of our minilesson. The challenge is to make these powerful and brief. A writer once wrote, "I am sorry I wrote such a long letter. I didn't have time to write a short one," and this sheds light on minilessons.

There are a few predictable challenges to keep in mind when planning the teaching component of a minilesson:

- *Teach in ways that move students along a gradient of difficulty as writers.* This requires an understanding of what most of our students can almost (but not quite) do, and it requires that the content we teach is multilevel enough to be useful and accessible for a wide range of writers.
- *Plan the method as well as the content of our teaching.* There are four methods that we use over and over in all our minilessons and conferences. We select the method and slot the particulars of today's topic into the template for that method.
- *Show writers when and why they'll use what you teach.* We need to help writers know how and when and why to access the knowledge we've given them so they can use the technique, concept, or strategy on the run as they write.

TEACH IN WAYS THAT MOVE CHILDREN ALONG A GRADIENT OF DIFFICULTY Our job is to teach in ways that enable children to do good work. It isn't okay, therefore, to say, "I taught such and such, but my kids are all struggling learners, so most of them can't do it." Our job is to plan a learning journey that ensures that all our children are productively engaged (which means they must be having some success and encountering some difficulties). If a teacher teaches something and children can't or don't grapple with what's been taught, then chances are the teacher didn't teach within the children's zone of proximal development.

Our job, as teachers, is to enable kids to do what they could not, at first, do. Often we will teach something in minilessons and then, as we move among youngsters, see that the words out of our mouths didn't magically transform all our five- and six-year-olds. When we find that our students can't do one thing or another, the skilled teacher thinks about how to better scaffold and support children. Tomorrow's minilesson grows out of our effort to scaffold children so that they grasp and can make use of whatever we are hoping to teach. This is what it means to hold ourselves accountable.

In the minilesson about using chunks to spell words, Abby's teaching was successful because she imagined a learning path for her students that was feasible for them. Her demonstration recruited her students to do something she believed that most of them could almost do. Most of Abby's children were already comfortable with the chunks she listed. She first demonstrated in a way that recruited children to join in with her while she listened for chunks in words. Then she nudged children to keep doing this a bit more while she was at their side. That is, she first scaffolded this work while the class was gathered together on the rug. Then she sent children off to continue doing more independently what she'd taught. The minilesson worked well, in part, because Abby planned a learning journey that was doable for her children, and she made the new work easy for them.

One way in which Abby made the work easy for her students was that she did some fancy footwork to avoid teaching ten things en route to her lesson on using word chunks. For example, because Abby's goal was *not* to show children how she sketches to plan ideas for a story, she skipped over this phase of writing altogether. Her goal also wasn't to teach children that there are words that we, as writers, know with automaticity. And

so she simply spelled words like "mom" easily, providing no oral commentary at all about them. Then, too, she went to some lengths to write a story filled with words that would give her many opportunities to put the day's lesson on letter chunks into practice.

Abby also made the lesson accessible to her students by keeping the instructions brief and clear. Abby's story about gymnastics was longer than the few sentences she incorporated into her minilesson, but after Abby had worked with three or four word chunks, she realized that her point had been made and that it was time to send children off to do their own writing. In the end, children do not learn to write from what *we* do but from their own efforts.

PLANNING THE METHOD AS WELL AS THE CONTENT OF OUR TEACHING It's crucial to keep in mind the difference between assigning and teaching. Abby could have said simply, "When you get to a tricky word, think about whether you know how to spell chunks of that word." But she knows that telling her students to do something—assigning—isn't teaching. Instead, Abby used one of four methods that we use over and over in our minilessons. In order to think about these methods of teaching, imagine that you want to teach someone to tie a special kind of knot. You could teach using any of these methods:

▸ Demonstration
▸ Explicitly tell and show an example
▸ Inquiry
▸ Guided practice

If you *demonstrated* to teach how to tie a knot, you'd start at the beginning; you'd go through the process step by step, talking aloud about each step as you progressed. Alternatively, you might decide to give a little illustrated talk about knot tying. If you were to *explicitly tell* about this knot tying, you'd try to make your talk memorable. Perhaps you'd consolidate the steps into a few main things to do and perhaps you'd use a metaphor, as I did when I taught my son how to tie his shoe by making bunny-ear loops. Almost certainly, you'd illustrate one or two steps along the way. Maybe you'd instead want to teach knot tying by using the method of *inquiry*, in which case you'd teach students that by looking closely at a knot, they can visibly discern its logic and figure out for themselves the directions that lie within the knot strings. Your goal in this lesson wouldn't just be for students to know the steps to tie that knot; instead, you'd teach them to become students of knots. You'd coach them to do this well ("Follow each rope with your eye—that's it!"). At the end of this lesson, you'd remind your students to use this inquiry process again to learn other things. Finally, you could hand out bits of rope and walk your students through the procedure using the methods of *guided practice*. "You saw me demonstrate. Try it and I'll coach into what you do. That's it, but remember that rope goes *behind*. . . ." One (or more) of these methods is used in every minilesson and conference.

Demonstrate: The Teaching Method Most Common in Minilessons

- Tell students how you hope they'll watch the demonstration, setting them up for what they'll soon be expected to know and/or do.

- Demonstrate what you hope the writers will soon be able to do. Think aloud as you demonstrate in ways that highlight whatever it is you hope students notice.
- Name again what you hope you've taught through demonstration.
- Usually, take the children to the beginning of the activity and help them get started doing what you have just demonstrated.

It is important to set up the demonstration so that students know what they should be paying attention to. For example, the teacher is apt to say, "I'm going to show you what happens when I'm writing a story and I come to words I don't know how to spell. Watch for—and list on your fingers— strategies I use when I come to hard words."

In a demonstration, we act out the very process we want our students to do. We don't *talk about* (or summarize) the activity or show the final results; instead, we reenact the blow-by-blow chronology of whatever it is we want our students to emulate.

As we demonstrate, we usually think aloud so that children can peek in on our thinking. In a demonstration, the teacher has to highlight the one aspect of the activity that she is trying to teach. And so if a teacher is trying to teach children strategies to use when they encounter words that are hard to spell, she won't fuss over her lead sentence or her use of dialogue. After the demonstration, the teacher usually debriefs students, pointing out what she hopes they noticed: "Did you see that I. . . ." Often the teacher then gets children started doing similar work. "So will you continue writing this sentence and when you come to a hard word, use these same strategies."

Explicitly Tell and Show an Example

- Explicitly tell students a concept you hope can guide them today and in the future. Teach them something interesting in a manner that will be memorable. Usually this means telling an anecdote or referring to a metaphor and usually it involves finding a memorable way to name what you are teaching. ("I want to teach you how to make small moments big.")
- Show the children an example to help them understand what you want them to do.
- Rename what you have taught.
- Help the writers get started doing what you have talked about.

There will be times (these are quite rare) when the teacher decides to explicitly teach students about something and to show an example. The challenge is to make this teaching informative and memorable. It helps to decide on the words you'll use as the "handles" for what you are trying to teach. The same activity could be described as "focusing in" or "zooming in" or "writing about a seed" or as "finding the most important part." Decide on one name you will give for whatever you are teaching and use that one name four or five times in the minilesson. Think of what you are doing as giving children a little speech on a topic. Ask, "What content can I put in my speech?" Will you share a few tips, tell an anecdote that ends up conveying a lesson, use a metaphor to teach a big idea? You'll want to think over how to make your teaching memorable. Perhaps you'll use an anecdote or a metaphor, parallel construction, or a gesture that represents your content. In any case, this method of teaching requires more (not less) planning than the others.

If your example includes citing a bit of children's literature, you need to consider how you'll highlight the aspect of that excerpt that is germane. Often you can bring one aspect into relief by using a case of contrast. Try saying, "This writer *could* have [just said, 'My dog is pretty,'] but instead he [said, 'My dog's eyes sparkled like. . . .']." Be sure your examples are very brief. Try to find examples that are within range of what the students should be reaching for and that don't illustrate twenty things at once. This method asks a great deal of a teacher.

Inquiry

- Invite children to join you in an inquiry.
- Demonstrate how you go about doing this inquiry.
- Engage the children in the inquiry, intervening to lift the level of what they do.
- Collect a small number of insights gleaned from the inquiry.
- Help children get started transferring these insights to their own writing.

This method is used rarely in minilessons designed for K–2 writers, and when it is used, it actually combines the methods of demonstration and guided practice. For example, if you want to help children notice the techniques an author uses to write, you demonstrate how you go about studying a page of a published author's text, finding something to admire, thinking about what the author did, and then naming it (that is, "dot, dot, dot"). Then you get children started inquiring in similar ways about the touchstone text. Be careful that in the name of inquiry you don't recruit children into making long lists of qualities of good writing. Otherwise, you end up listing and assigning in lieu of teaching.

Guided Practice

- Interject lean prompts to scaffold the child's work in a step-by-step fashion. (Your prompts can also lift the level of what the child is doing.)

- Let the intervals between your prompts become longer as the child becomes accustomed to the process and is able to continue with less support.

- Help the child start (or continue) so that he or she is working more independently. (For example, if the guided practice helped a child "write in the air," help the child get started putting this on the paper.)

During guided practice, we guide children so that they have an instructive experience that they wouldn't have been able to have on their own. First we engage the child in the activity, and then we use clear, efficient prompts (preferably ones the children have heard before and understand) to coach children as they progress along. The amount of scaffolding we provide lessens as children proceed with more independence. We hope that once the minilesson is over, children will be able to do the same processes without requiring our support.

When we guide children to do something in their mind's eye or orally, we then hope that they will soon turn around and do this same work in their writing. Once we've completed a bit of guided practice, children will be at the end of the action (and the close of the story) and need us to take them back to the start and set them up so that they can do the same set of actions, this time without our help.

SHOW WRITERS WHEN AND WHY THEY'LL USE WHAT YOU TEACH Minilessons are rather like the huddles in the midst of a football game or roll call at the police station at the start of Hill Street Blues, or like the gathering of art students around one person's easel. Each of these gatherings contains a mix of informality, clarity, and urgency. And in each of these instances, the learners have been and will continue to be involved in an activity. In each instance, the leader says, "I've been watching you as you work and I have one tip that may help you as you continue your work."

The fact that we use the minilesson format to teach writers *who are in the midst of* writing changes the content of what we teach. In minilessons, we are usually trying to convey methods and strategies—and we situate whatever we teach inside the story of someone's ongoing work. We may say, "When I write . . ." or "When you are writing . . ." or "If you are writing and you. . . ."

Sometimes when I see a teacher struggle with minilessons, the problem stems from the teacher's regarding the minilesson as a time to lay out some information about the English language rather than as a time to give writers a tip they can use as they write. The difference between the two is subtle—but significant. A minilesson is not a forum for laying out information about the English language. A minilesson *is* a forum for giving young writers a tip, suggestion, or model for how they can improve their practice.

Minilesson Teaching: Information *and* a Tip

Instead of teaching only a bit of information . . .	I try to teach strategies . . .
Writers leave spaces between their words.	When you are sounding out a word and you come to the place where there are no more sounds, that's the end of the word. Leave a little space—a resting place—then go to the next word.
Nonfiction texts contain certain features (table of contents, subheads, captions).	When writing nonfiction on a big topic, it helps to plan out the different subtopics you might address, and to list those in a table of contents that might look like this (show one). Then, inside any one chapter, it helps to plan out the different subtopics and to almost make little chapters—or subsections—inside that chapter.
In a focused text, every section of the text develops the main idea.	When we write, we often think first of a very big topic (getting a dog, for example). Before we actually start writing, however, it helps to think, "What are the particular parts (or incidents) within that big topic?" After listing these, we often choose just one as the focused topic for our text (for example, getting a dog is like getting a new brother). Then every paragraph addresses that one focused idea.

Active Engagement

We set children up to briefly use the strategy or concept we've tried to teach them.

Children learn more from what they do than from the words out of someone else's mouth. Therefore, after we teach something, we try to engineer things so that children have a few minutes to try whatever we've just taught them.

With older children—third- and fourth-graders, for example—we can demonstrate a strategy using our own draft and then suggest that students take a minute or two, while sitting with us on the rug, to transfer that strategy to their own writing. "Sometimes I reread my drafts thinking, 'Are there places where I could make my characters talk?'" we might say to older children, and show how we have starred one such place in our own draft and then wrote some dialogue to insert into that place. Then with these older writers, we might say, "Could partners one and two look at partner two's draft and see if you can find a place where it'd help if you made a character talk? Put a mark at that place in the draft and say out loud to each other what you'd actually insert into that draft." Instructions such as these would probably be out of reach for most K–2 kids. (It's not that five- and six-year-olds can't make characters talk, especially if they do so by adding speech balloons into their illustrations. But even though most children could add a speech balloon and some words into their drawings, it would be ambitious to expect that within the fast pace of a minilesson, a whole class of kindergarten or early first graders could each pull out his or her ongoing writing, reread or otherwise recall the content, locate a section that could profit from dialogue, and tell a friend the specific words to add! The process would be time-consuming and the logistics, overwhelming.) Therefore, we're more apt to set young children up to practice a strategy within a shared text, as Abby did when she set her kindergartners up to think about the chunks they knew in two words—*handstands* and *sat*—from Abby's gymnastics story. If Abby, instead, had been teaching children that writers can make their characters talk, she could have set children up to each tell their partner what they might make a particular character say within a shared story.

As I mentioned earlier, when we want children to do some work around a shared text, it's ideal to use a story we (or the class) have written about a shared topic. This way the story is equally available to everyone. Perhaps the hamster has escaped the day before. At home, I might write a scanty, underdeveloped text about the event and come to the minilesson asking for help. I'd have written a story that resembles ones children are apt to write (although unless we are highlighting spelling, we usually spell correctly). I could begin the minilesson telling children that after I have written a story, I always reread it and think, "What did I leave out?" Then I could say, "So I'll reread a story I wrote last night. Could you join me in thinking, 'Is there more to add?'" Then I read aloud, as if I'm a writer rereading and envisioning my story.

We looked and looked. Then Robert saw some hamster food. We knew we were close. We found him behind the bookcase. We put him in the cage.

"I'm remembering that time, aren't you? Do you guys remember how Robert pointed to the food and said, 'He was here!'" Then I would say to the class, "Let's add that." As an aside I mention that writers do just what we are doing. They reread and sometimes remember the words a character *actually said* and then add those exact words. Then I either use a carat to insert the dialogue or, for younger children, draw a speech balloon over Robert's head, filling it with "He was here!" "Let's keep reading and see if there are any other places where we

could make characters talk," I'd say. Then I'd read "We found him behind the bookcase" with an intonation that suggests that we could *definitely* make a character talk at this crucial junction. "Tell your partner what we might have said when we saw him," I say, giving everyone a chance to try their hand at telling a partner how they'd add some dialogue into the whole-class text. Soon I will have elicited one person's suggestion and added it to the text (I *don't* elicit a whole slew of suggestions).

The episode above shows how we shift between teaching and active involvement and also shows how we can provide a great deal of scaffolding for children's active involvement. During the next day's minilesson, we might want to do almost the same minilesson with a different text, and this time we'd try to provide children with a bit less scaffolding. We might say, "I've really gotten excited about making my characters talk and I've been rereading old pieces from long ago and thinking, 'Could I add talk to this one?' Sometimes I can't remember what people *really* said, so I just make up what they *might have said*. Let's try it together with this story. You remember, it was about when the toilet overflowed and came leaking into our room. I'm going to read *the whole story* without stopping—you can follow with your eyes—and then I'll ask you and your partner to find one place where you could make people talk. If you don't remember exactly what we said that day, you can think, 'What did we probably say?' Okay?" In the previous lesson, *I* was the one to locate a place that could contain added dialogue. In this minilesson, children are asked to locate a place for dialogue on their own.

There are other ways to support young children's efforts to become actively involved doing the minilesson. For example, we might:

▶ *Do something and ask children to be researchers, articulating what we did*. "Tell your partner what you saw me doing that you could do too," we could say. In a similar fashion, we could ask children to watch other children or study what an author has done and in either instance, they could tell each other what they noticed the writer doing that was worth emulating.

▶ *Ask children to try it immediately.* If the teaching component of our minilesson has taught children something that writers do, we could tell children, "Get started doing that right now, while you're on the carpet. When I see that you have a good start, I'll send you back to your writing spot to continue."

▶ *Ask children to plan to do it immediately*. If the teaching component of our minilesson has taught children something that writers do, we could ask children to plan for how they'll do that in their writing. Specifically, we could ask them to reread their writing and find a place where they could do that same thing. "Mark it with a planning sticky note that reminds you of your plans." Once children have found and marked the place to do the proposed work, we can send them off. Alternatively, we could suggest that children tell their partner their plans.

There are a few predictable problems we encounter during the active involvement phase of a minilesson. First, children can spend all their time on the logistics of this and never do the work. "You go first," one will say to her partner. "No, you," the other responds. "No, you." Similarly, one child will push his paper toward the other

child, and this time the back and forth will be, "You read it." "No, *you* read it." Teachers need to expect problems like these and realize that the minilesson structure can be used to teach children how to participate well in a writing workshop. We usually treat these logistical details as part of the important work of learning what good writers do. "Writers don't waste one precious minute of their partner time," we may say. "Watch me and my partner," we say, roping in a student teacher. Perhaps we reenact some of the horseplay we have seen kids doing with *their* partners. "Does *this* look like we're making smart use of our partner time?" Children will chorus, "Noooo." Then, for contrast, we can say, "Now watch me and my partner," and this time we look our partner in the eyes, nod responsively as he or she talks, and so forth. We might make little asides as we do this, muttering, "Oh, what a great question! I love that question she asked!" or "Don't you love how she listens? I feel like she's really interested."

During this stage of a minilesson, as in every other stage, the greatest risk is that the *mini*lesson will become a *maxi*lesson, and that children won't, therefore, have thirty or forty minutes in which to actually write. Often the active involvement a teacher has planned can't possibly fit into a few minutes. Equally often, a teacher will act as if the active involvement is only worthwhile if each child reports back to the whole group on what he or she has done. Some teachers go so far as to think that each child not only needs to report to classmates but that the teacher also needs to record each child's contributions on chart paper. This truly creates problems!

In general, a teacher needs to remember that just as assigning isn't teaching, so too recording something on chart paper isn't teaching. If a teacher wants to add one or two one-line items to a chart during a minilesson, that's sensible. After a minilesson on the strategy of revising a text by making characters talk, for example, a teacher might add this item onto a list of revision strategies. But it would be a waste of time to have fifteen children report back on the ways they would revise the story of the hamster search, and for the teacher to carefully scribe every single contribution! If one, two, or *at the most* three children share their ideas, the class will have more than enough examples dancing in their heads, and it'll be time to send them off to write.

Link

> We restate our teaching point and either try to ensure that every child applies this new learning to their ongoing work today, or encourage children to add today's teaching point to their repertoire of possible strategies or goals.

Pulitzer-prize-winning writer Donald Murray once told me that the single most important sentence in a paragraph is the last one. "This sentence needs to propel readers onward to the next paragraph," he said. "It needs to be not a closing, but a launch." I remember this advice when I reach the final bend in my minilessons. These last few sentences need to encapsulate the content of the minilesson in such a way that kids get their hands around it and carry it with them as they head off from whole-class, teacher-led work into the whole of their writing lives.

The challenge to teach in a way that makes a real difference is not for the faint of heart. It's a tall order indeed to believe that we can call children together into a huddle, take five minutes to teach a technique, and they'll then actually add that technique to their repertoire, using it when the time is right.

And so we speak with great energy. "And so I'm hoping that *today* and *every day*," we say, and we say this with great solemnity, knowing this repeating phrase may matter more than anything else in our teaching. "You'll take time to reread your work and to ask, 'Does this make sense?' If it doesn't make sense, class, what do writers do?"

"Fix it!"

"That's so smart of you. Thumbs up if you are quite sure that from this day onward, you'll be the kind of writer who rereads your own work and asks, 'Does that make sense?' All of you?! Wow. That is so cool. The writers who are seated at the blue table can get started. At the green table. . . ."

I try to remember four things when I plan the link between my minilesson and writing time:

- *Crystallize the lesson*. I consolidate the lesson into a clear, even catchy phrase that will be easy for children to hold onto and remember. I may repeat the key phrases several times during the last minute of the minilesson, and I know I'll weave these phrases into future conferences and minilessons. The key phrase in the minilesson might be, "Writers look with honest eyes," or "Remember, you are not just a writer, you are a writing teacher," or "Writers show, not tell," or "Take a small moment and make it big," or "Writers add, and writers subtract," or "Let Eve Bunting be your writing teacher." Whatever it is, I find ways to repeat those words so they become a song in children's minds.

▸ *Generalize the lesson*. As today's lesson ends, I want children to remember that today's minilesson is for every day's writing. Sometimes I'll make sure everyone uses the tool I've taught today, but just as often I'll want children to use the tool only when they need it. Either way, however, I need to remind children that the lesson is for "today, and every day" and that "from this day onward" they'll need to remember this tool. Sometimes it helps to put the lesson onto a chart where today's lesson lasts and cumulates alongside others. Such charts might be titled, "How Writers Revise," "Finding Topics for Writing," "When Writers Are Done, They've Just Begun," "What Good Writing Teachers Do," "Qualities of Good Writing," or "Lessons Mem Fox Can Teach Us." It is also important that teachers move between specific examples and general principles. If the minilesson has been geared toward teaching one new trick for turning narratives into poems, I'll want to say, "So you can do *any* of these things when you want to turn a narrative into a poem," and then I'll reread the whole list, adding the new item.

▸ *Make the transitions smooth*. It's worth my time to think about how to expediently move my twenty-five kids from the carpet and to their workstations. It's worthwhile to develop and refine a system that will then remain in place almost every day. If the system is always changing, it becomes forefront in children's

minds and in our own, and at this crucial juncture, our hope is that children's minds are on their writing topics and plans.

▸ *Boost the children's writing energy*. Don Murray once said, "Above all, in a writing conference, the writer's energy for writing needs to go up, not down." The same can be true for the link. Above all, it needs to boost children's energy for writing, not sap it.

Tips for Minilessons:

Make connections short and beyond the obvious.

The first phase of a minilesson, the connection, is the place to reiterate the key point from yesterday in a way that contextualizes today's work. But you need to avoid restating the obvious. You don't need to say, "We've been studying poetry." If, so far, you've learned five ways to revise poems, you certainly don't need to repeat all five of these ways. Get to the point: "Yesterday we added one final revision strategy to our list—we said poets do such and such. Today I want to warn you that these revisions don't *always* improve a poem."

Don't over-rely on charts.

Often your minilessons will lead you to create charts that become a permanent reminder of your instruction. Be careful not to fool yourself into thinking, however, that writing something on a chart suffices as a way to make your teaching memorable. Writing on the chart can be a way to *record* your teaching, but it can't substitute for teaching. A rule of thumb is to be sure your minilesson would be rich without writing on the chart and be sure you spend no more than 5% of your minilesson time doing this writing. A chart that lists five strategies will usually record more than a week (not one day) of minilessons.

Limit examples.

Sometimes we use too many examples when one or two would suffice. Don't let examples overwhelm your point. If you want to show the value of adding dialogue and you are going to read aloud two drafts, one that has dialogue and one that doesn't, the drafts shouldn't be full of a million other commendable qualities that distract from your point.

Help children's contributions matter.

If you call on a child in a minilesson, that child's contribution needs to be as important to the class as your words are. Make sure children turn and look at the speaker. "Eyes on Carl," you'll say.

Use concrete visuals.

Whenever possible, it helps to make your minilesson concrete. If you are going to mention three familiar books, it's great to hold each as you say the book's title. If you are going to talk about tiny, tiny details, use hand gestures to show just how tiny those details are.

Limit children's contributions.

There are predictable places where minilessons get derailed. One of these is at the end of the active involvement, after children have talked to or worked with their partners. Often teachers get seduced into hearing a huge number of children report back what they said to partners. If you need any children to report back (which shouldn't be a foregone conclusion), you'll usually benefit from calling on only one or two children and then responding to their comments so that this becomes an extension of your teaching time. The reporting back needs to serve the good of the class, not function only as a private conversation between you and the child you called on.

Use familiar texts.

It would be rare to read aloud a brand-new text as part of a minilesson. There are a number of reasons why we instead are apt to reread familiar texts in a minilesson. First, children deserve the chance to encounter a text first as simply an appreciative reader, without being told, "Listen for the action words in this story." Then, too, once a child knows a text as a reader of it, it makes sense to look at the text and ask, "How did the author make this?" Finally, the minilesson is usually about one aspect of a text only, so it makes sense to zero in on a section of the text only; this works better if the entire text is one children know very well.

Make your directions clear and consistent.

There are two places in a minilesson where we ask kids to do some work. One is at the start of active engagement; the other is in the link. In both these places, the teacher must give directions and they need to be crystal clear. It helps if the vocabulary of these sections is consistent. In hundreds of minilessons, teachers will say, "Turn and talk to your partner about . . ."; soon children do this effortlessly. Don't vary the wording on this or other directions.

Demonstrate often.

Remember that the qualities of good writing are often the qualities of good teaching. The injunction to "show, not tell" applies to teachers as well as writers. Whenever a teacher has the choice between demonstrating or explaining, the former is preferable. And if you want children to remember an injunction, make it *detailed*, not general.

Offer contrasts.

It often helps to role-play exaggerated versions of what not to do. For example, I might tell children, "Sometimes my writing friend makes me feel awful. Let me show you," and I proceed to reenact a listener who yawns, look past the writer to see out the window, acts bored, and does every other bad thing imaginable. Children will laugh with delight—but the message hits home.

CONFERRING WITH YOUNG WRITERS

Recently, school leaders from Tampa Pinellas County asked me, "What are the behaviors you look for in good teachers of reading and writing?" I answered that first, I want teachers to understand that when we teach writing, we are teaching young people to do something. When we teach someone to do anything—whether it's to play the oboe, to swim, to make pottery—the learner needs to be doing the thing, and we, as teachers, need to establish structures within which learners do the work. And then I said that we, as teachers, need to hold ourselves accountable for learners doing good work. Our job is to design the curriculum so that over time, we set learners up for success at more and more challenging enterprises. Just as we first help children read very supportive books well and then we move them onto more challenging texts, we also need to design the curriculum so that writers move along.

Finally, we need to coach into what children do so that we help them make great strides as learners. In the teaching of primary writing, the quality of work that children do has everything to do with the teaching they receive.

After looking at some of the writing I included in this series, a teacher recently said to me, "My second graders don't write as well as those kindergartners." I think she wanted me to sympathize with her unlucky lot in life. I was silent. What I wanted to tell her was that good teaching matters.

When we give children rich environments for learning to write *and* wise, assertive one-to-one coaching, children regularly produce work that is breathtaking. The good news is that the skills of strong teaching are within reach for us all. Over the decades, I have watched literally thousands of teachers become more skilled as teachers of writing. The process is a self-sustaining one because as teachers become more skilled, their children respond with small miracles. And this time when we see good writing, we know the explanation lies not in a child's genes but in the instruction the child has received. When we give children both rich, rigorous learning environments and direct, intimate one-to-one coaching, we tap an extraordinary source of power.

Although conferences *appear* to be warm, informal conversations, they are in fact highly principled teaching interactions, carefully designed to move writers along learning pathways.

In this chapter, I hope to elucidate the principles that guide me, and others, as we confer with young writers. Specifically, I'll discuss:

- The variety of conferences. I'll suggest that it is helpful to think about three overlapping kinds of conferences.
- The architecture of writing conferences. I'll suggest that there are four components of a conference, each with its own challenges.

THE VARIETY OF CONFERENCES

Almost every conference is structured similarly, with a teacher researching, then deciding what and how to teach, then teaching. Conferences end with a link to children's ongoing work.

Although conferences almost all follow this same architecture, there are categories of conferences, and each kind of conference has its own character:

- Content conferences
- Expectation conferences
- Process and goals conferences

Content Conferences

"I didn't realize you braid your sister's hair! Tell me all about it. What happens first?"

At the start of the year, primary teachers conduct many content conferences. Then we tend to find that children can provide this sort of support for one another and for themselves, so we shift to more process and goals conferences.

In a content conference, we learn the content of the child's writing and decide that the child needs our help developing (or elaborating on) this content. Usually we decide to give the child guided practice at telling his or her content. We get the child started saying what he or she will write and then interject lean prompts ("How did it start?" "Really? Say more about that." "What exactly did you do?") to elicit more content.

In our interjections, we alternate between being responsive to what the child says, saying back what we've heard, and prompting the child for more detail.

After eliciting more elaborate content, we nudge the child to record what he or she has said onto the paper. Children usually profit from our taking them back to the start of their story or their points and then getting them started writing with new detail. We may simply praise what the child has done in his or her oral version ("You told this with so much detail! I can picture it") and then move on, or we may support this writing through guided practice in which we continue to interject prompts meant to elicit detail.

Expectation Conferences

"Mario, do you think Maurice Sendak turns his stories into airplanes? He doesn't. Writers keep their writing in folders."

Early in the year, it is important to induct children into the norms of a writing workshop. If a child is running around the room during writing time or preventing other children from working or copying rather than writing, we hold an expectation conference. In these conferences, the research phase is usually brief. We observe the child doing something, perhaps interview to learn a tiny bit about what the child thinks he or she is doing, and then we decide to redirect the writer. We do this by clearly and explicitly communicating what we've seen the child doing and what we expect to see in a writing workshop. "Eric Carle

doesn't waste his precious writing time running round the room," we're apt to say. "And you are not going to do that either."

Then we help the child get started doing what we hope the child will do. That is, we may move the child to a new writing spot, take away the pointer/sword, get the child to pick up his pencil, etc.

Often, at this point, we shift into another kind of conference to support the child as he or she gathers momentum on the more productive activity. Often, then, expectation conferences are double-decker ones, shifting to become also content or process and goals conferences.

Process and Goals Conferences

"I notice you told what Sammy looks like. That was smart. Another way to help us know Sammy—or any character—is to include the exact words the character says. What I do is I reread and then I pause and think, 'What did he probably say?' Watch. I'll show you."

Initially we thought this final category could be divided in half, with some conferences designed to teach children a new strategy, others to help them reach for a new goal. But the truth is that strategies are strategies (rather than activities) only when they are used toward a goal. Writers don't just add to a draft by inserting flaps; they add inserted text *so as to* bring characters to life, build the tension in their story, show the setting, tell the internal story, and so on. Similarly, if a child learns goals (writing with sensory details, for example) without strategies, this too is useless. Why learn the characteristics of a good ending or the fact that readable writing has spaces between the words without learning strategies for achieving these goals?

The vast majority of effective conferences are process and goals conferences. In these conferences, a teacher learns the process and goals that are already in play for a child and then teaches in ways that lift the level or alter those processes and goals.

THE ARCHITECTURE OF WRITING CONFERENCES

Writing conferences are conversations between a learner and a coach. These conversations are intimate and infinitely varied. As true as this is, the opposite is also true. One writing conference is also very similar to another. Writing conferences assume that writers are first engaged in their own work as writers. That is, we must first organize and teach the whole class in such a way that each child is engaged in his or her own purposeful work as a writer. Then we observe and coach in ways that either help the child better do what the child is trying to do or direct the child to take on new (and perhaps more challenging) intentions. Either way, we generally need to briefly scaffold the higher-level work

that a child does. Then we pull back, encouraging the child to continue without relying on us as much. This means that a writing conference almost always involves these components:

Research what the child is intending to do and has done.

Decide what to teach and how to teach it

Teach using one of four methods, each of which usually ends in guided practice.

Link by extrapolating from today's work whatever it is that the writer will want to carry forward into tomorrow's work.

The predictability of these interactions makes them more powerful because it allows teachers and children to assimilate what they learn from prior conferences and carry those lessons with them and because it allows teachers and children to anticipate and plan for future conferences.

Research

Observe and interview to understand what the child is trying to do as a writer.

When we teach writers of any age, we need to first learn what the writer is already trying to do. The research phase, then, begins with a teacher observing, interviewing, and sometimes reading the child's work in order to understand what the child is intending to do as a writer. Let me explain why this matters. The conferences we hold with children about their writing are not unlike the interactions principals and staff developers have with *us* about our teaching. It's helpful if the person who coaches *us* first listens and observes to learn what we are already trying to do.

Imagine, for example, that we had already spent months focusing on the strugglers in our classroom, and we decided now to nudge our strongest students to do better work. What if an administrator sat in on a few moments of our teaching and blithely told us that we mustn't focus on our strong students at the expense of our strugglers! If that administrator had prefaced his or her visit by asking, "What have you been working on?" and, "How's it been going?" and even, "So can I watch that?" *then* the coaching interventions could either help us do what we were already trying to do or (if the coach questioned our intentions) lead us to reevaluate the rationale behind our intentions ("I can see you have been working on X, but I want to urge you to work also [or instead] on Y"). Then the coach would help us understand what informed his or her judgment, and we'd be off and running.

Because it is crucial to learn about a writer's intention, we almost always begin a conference with older children by asking the writer to articulate what he or she is working on. "What are you working on as a writer?" we ask, and we teach children that when they respond to this question, we want to learn not just the writer's content ("my dog") or genre and content ("a poem about my dog") but also the writer's goals and strategies ("I'm writing a poem about my dog *and I'm trying to be sure readers can visualize my dog so I'm adding more descriptive words*"). Even though young children will not always be able to give us a detailed description of their writing agendas, we still need to give them opportunities to put their intentions into words. Often, then, even when conferring with a five- or six-year-old, we'll begin a conference by asking, "What are you working on as a writer?"

However, because young children won't always be able to name their intentions, we are especially careful to observe and examine their writing with an eye toward piecing together the child's intentions. Often, we'll say back what it is that we see the child doing, thereby giving the child words he or she can eventually use to articulate his or her intentions. We may, for example, say "I'm noticing that you are revising. It looks like you are adding details onto the main part—the most important thing—in your story. Is that right?"

In the research component of a conference, then, the teacher observes, interviews, and sometimes studies the child's writing in order to understand what the child is trying to do as a writer. We usually begin by watching from a distance, noticing especially the writer's engagement in his or her writing. Then we draw close and continue watching, using this glimpse of the child at work to help us begin to understand the child's process as a writer.

Probe in order to understand more about the child's intentions.

Usually once a child has told us what he or she is trying to do, we probe in order to understand what the child means. If the child says, "I'm revising to show, not tell," we are apt to say, "Can you show me where you did that?" or "What do you mean by this change here?" Of course, we usually understand the terms children use (because they give us back the very terms we've taught them), but it is crucial to help a child articulate what he or she means by "I'm revising" or "I'm fixing up my ending." Sometimes we tell children what we notice, speculate about their intentions, and ask for their confirmation.

Name what the child has done as a writer and remind him or her to do this often in future writing.

As we do this, we are thinking first, "What has the child done—or gestured toward doing—that I could name and make a fuss over?" Early on in our interactions with a child, we spot something that the child has done (or has almost done) that has significance in the child's learning journey, and we name this in a way we hope makes it likely that the child will do this same wise work again in future pieces of writing. The trick is that we need to be able to extrapolate something transferable out of the details of the child's work. If the child added the sound her guinea pig makes when it squeaks into her draft, we don't say, "I love that you added the 'ee, ee, ee' sound to your story. I hope you add that squeaking sound into your stories often!" Instead, we name what the child has done in a way that makes the action replicable: "I love the way you reread and added teeny details that could help readers create movies in their minds of exactly what happened. You made it so I can picture your guinea pig. Whenever you write, add details like these." Or, "I love the way you've brought out dialogue—even if it is guinea pig dialogue! You didn't just say, 'Freddy made noises to greet me,' you told us exactly what he said!"

Decide/Teach

As we observe, interview and read the child's work, we're thinking, thinking, thinking. As I mentioned earlier, we're thinking first, "What has the child done that I can name and celebrate?" But we're especially thinking, "Of all that I could teach the child, what might make the biggest difference right now?"

In deciding what to teach, we draw on these considerations:

▶ If possible, we equip the child to do what it is he or she intends to do. If we don't want to get behind the child's existing intentions (or if we can't discern what these are), we try to rally the child to take on a new intention *and then* we equip the child to realize that intention. That is, if a child is writing in generalizations, we could simply elicit details and get the child to record them. We try *not* to do that, but rather we first teach the child that writers write with details, rallying the child behind the importance of that goal. *Then* we can proceed to elicit those details and get them recorded on the page.

▶ We're always teaching toward independence—and growth. We try to decide on an intervention that will extend what the child can already do but also to teach within the child's reach so that what the child does with our support today, he or she can do independently tomorrow.

▶ We are always informed by our goals. These goals come from an overall sense of what we value in writers (well-structured stories, growing control of conventions, a readiness to emulate other authors, and so on) and learners (initiative, zeal, skills, a willingness to take risks and to work hard, self-awareness, and so on) and from the specific goals we have in mind for a unit of study and for a child.

During the "decide" phase of a conference, we decide not only *what* but also *how* we will teach. We teach using one (and sometimes more than one) of the four methods described in the minilesson chapter:

▶ Guided practice
▶ Demonstration
▶ Explicitly tell and show examples
▶ Inquiry

For example, imagine that I noticed Andrew reread his draft. He reread:

> I brought my new puppy home in the car.
> I named him Ruffy.
> We played a lot.

Then Andrew inserted a carat after his first sentence and added, "I loved him so, so, so, much!"

"I notice you are revising, Andrew," I'd say, "What are you trying to do?"

Andrew would presumably say, "I want to show how much I loved my puppy, because I really did love him."

At this point, I could decide to teach Andrew that when writers want to convey a feeling, they don't always tell the feeling straight out. Sometimes, instead, they use other writerly techniques to convey the feeling. I could make this teaching point using any one of four methods.

ONE OPTION: TEACH BY INQUIRY "I can see, Andrew, that you really want us to feel how much you loved your puppy! One thing I do when I really want to convey a strong feeling to my readers is, I study how other writers manage to do this. Remember yesterday when we read *Koala Lou*? Mem Fox wanted us to know that Koala Lou really, really, really wanted to win that race. Let's open *Koala Lou* to that part and notice how Mem Fox helped us realize what Koala Lou felt. Hmmm. What do you notice on this page?"

"Well," Andrew said, "she really wanted to win."

"Point to the place on the page that shows that."
He did.

"What is Mem Fox doing to help you understand how much Koala Lou wanted to win?"

"She tells details."

"Can you say more? What exactly is Mem Fox doing?"

"She tells us how Koala Lou acted at the race, like how she watched the other Koala and worried and all."

"That's smart! So you're noticing that Mem Fox helped us know Koala Lou's feelings by showing details of how exactly she acted out those feelings. Are you thinking *you* might use details that show exactly how you acted out your love of that puppy?"

ANOTHER OPTION: TEACH BY EXPLICITLY TELLING AND SHOWING AN EXAMPLE "I can see, Andrew, that you really want us to feel how much you loved your puppy. When writers want to convey strong feelings, we often follow a very important writing rule. It's this: Show, don't tell. A famous writer, Mark Twain, put it this way: 'Don't say the old lady yelled. Put her on the stage and have her yell.'"

"So when Cynthia Rylant wrote *The Relatives Came*, she took that advice. She didn't say, 'We love each other.' She just put the relatives in the house and had them loving each other. Remember?"

> *Then it was hugging time. Talk about hugging! Those relatives just passed us all around their car, pulling us against their wrinkled Virginia clothes, crying sometimes. They hugged us for hours.*

"I'm thinking in your story, you could take the same advice. Don't say, 'I loved that puppy.' Just get in the car with that puppy on the way home from the SPCA and start loving him. What exactly did you do? That's what it means to show, not tell."

"Well, I patted him and said stuff."

"So tell me, bit by bit. 'I got in the car.' Then what?" (*This is now guided practice.*)

"I got in the car. I had the box on my lap. I heard him scratch, so I said, 'We'll be there soon.'"
"You got it! That's showing. Put that down: 'I got in the car. . . .'"

ANOTHER OPTION: TEACH BY DEMONSTRATION "I can see, Andrew, that you really want us to feel how much you loved your puppy. When writers want to convey strong feelings, we often follow one very important writing rule. It's this: Show, don't tell. What that means is we show something, rather than telling it. So let's pretend I'd written:"

> I brought my new
> puppy home in the car.
> I was very very
> scared of him.

"And let's say I decided to follow that show-not-tell rule. Watch what I do. Notice there are three steps."

I gestured, step one. "Let me first reread this and see *where* I need to show, not tell. Oops—here! Where it says, 'I was very very scared of the puppy.' I can *show* that."

I gestured, step two. "Okay. Let me remember getting in the car with the puppy and sitting with him. I want to get that feeling of being scared in me again and act out just what I did. I pushed the box far away from me on the seat. 'Now you can't bite me,' I said. I heard him scratch on the side of the box. I turned my back to the box, and put my coat over my head so I didn't hear the scratches."

Turning to Andrew, I named what I'd just done. "Did you see how *first* [I gesture with one finger] I found the place where I needed to show the feeling and *second* [I gesture to show this is second on the list] I got the feeling in me and remembered the exact time when I felt it? I sort of acted out how it went, and said what happened that showed how scared I was. Now [I indicate this would be third] I'd have to write that down."

"But you weren't scared of your puppy, were you? You loved him. So what you need to do as a writer to show, not tell, that feeling of loving your puppy is, first, you need to reread and find where you could show your feelings of loving the puppy. Do that while I watch." (*Again this now shifts into Guided Practice.*)

ANOTHER OPTION: TEACH BY GUIDED PRACTICE "I can see, Andrew, that you really want us to feel how much you loved your puppy. When writers want to convey strong feelings, we often follow one very important writing rule. It's this: Show, don't tell. What that means is we show something rather than telling it. What you need to do is to get the feeling of loving your puppy inside you right now. Do you have it?"

Andrew nodded.

"Pretend you're feeling that love, and you get in the car with the puppy. Was it in a box?"

"Yeah."

"Okay. So you sort of need to act out how it went. Hold the pretend box. Show me where you put the box."

Andrew indicated that he held the box on his lap.

"Now show me what you said or did on the ride and how that came from loving your puppy."

"That I took it out?"

"Show me what happened exactly. You're holding the box—do that. Now what happened?"

"He was scratching, so I said, 'Don't worry little guy,' but he cried, so I got him on my lap and he went under my coat."

"Andrew, what you are doing right now is just what writers do when we want to show, not tell. We almost act the time out in our minds just like you are doing, and we say all the little exact things we do; then we write that down. So will you start, 'I got in the car and held the box. I heard my puppy scratching.' Write that."

CHAPTER 7

SUPPORTING ENGLISH LANGUAGE LEARNERS

No suggestions for second language learners can encompass all the myriad needs of each individual child. That said, there are a few general rules that apply to the fundamentals of teaching second language learners. Above all, a teacher must know whether a child is literate in his or her first language.

English language learners with high literacy skills in their first language will predictably go through a series of stages when learning English, but they will pick up English very quickly, especially if they are receiving a lot of language input by being included in conversations and interactions. If a child is literate in his first language and in his silent, or early production, phase in learning English, the teacher will want to encourage this child to write in his first language and then to label the accompanying picture in English. The rationale for asking this child to write in his first language is this: If a child can't speak in English, the child will not be able to write in English. Before long, however, this child will be in an intermediate stage of learning English, and at this point the child can certainly write in English. Even when they can write in English, however, children who are literate in their first language should be encouraged to write in their native language at times also. This will support the child's ability to write in English—literacy skills are transferable. In general, children with high literacy skills in their first language will not need as much scaffolding as children who are not yet literate in their first language.

Offer More Chances for Speaking and Listening

In order to develop English language skills, all English language learners need good linguistic models in English. For these children, it is particularly essential that the teacher create many, many opportunities for conversation. If a K–1 teacher has many ELL students, she will probably want to have a choice time each day so that children build with blocks or legos, improvise with puppets, re-create grocery stores and banks, and the like. The teacher can think of each area—the blocks, the puppets, and so forth—as a forum for supporting a particular language function. "Here, in the block area, I will get children explaining to each other what they have built," the teacher might plan. "Here, in the dramatic play area, I will get children taking on the voices of characters and re-creating stories."

The teacher may want to start each day by inviting grown-ups of all sorts into the room—paraprofessionals, parents, reading support teachers, and the like—and having these adults meet with small clusters of children to help them retell and discuss what they did at home the evening before.

Although it is crucial to plan special occasions that invite conversation, the most important thing is to be sure that conversations occur all day long and that many of the conversations are child-to-child (not the teacher calling on one child after another while the whole class looks on). Above all, it is simply not acceptable for the child who doesn't speak English to work and learn in isolation. Too often a teacher will gesture to a child on the margins of the room and say, "Leave her be—she speaks Korean." If one child speaks Korean, we probably need to find another Korean speaker to converse with that child. The simplest solution is to ask, "Does anyone speak Korean?" It helps to partner children and to engineer partnerships so that children who have more and less language proficiency are partnered with each other. It may be that some partnerships need to be trios. And if a child in the classroom speaks a language that no one else does, at the very least she or he needs to be a part of a small interactive unit like everyone else.

The important principle to keep in mind is that English language learners need more, not fewer, interactions with us and with others. It is understandable why teachers sometimes steer around children who don't speak English, but we simply can't let the fact that we feel helpless or awkward prevent us from interacting with our English language learners *more* than we interact with our other students. We needn't speak the child's language nor be skilled communicators. We may just point at the child's picture: "Is that you?" (A nod.) "Is that the slide? Wow!" Gestures will help, but what is most important is our presence at the child's side and our attentiveness to the child.

It's okay to blunder along, interacting with English language learners as best we can, but there is another crucial thing to keep in mind: Wait. When talking with English language learners, it is easy to feel uncomfortable when there are long pauses and to jump in to answer our own questions. This teaches children that if they are passive and silent for a bit, we will take over. We need to let the long pauses happen and avoid jumping in too quickly. After waiting for a minute, it may help to rephrase the question before again giving the child time to answer. Children have a lot of processing to do, and this can't happen instantly. Give them a chance to think. Allow for dramatic pauses. You ask, "Who is this in your picture?" Finally, if need be, you can step in and demonstrate the sort of answer you were expecting. Wait the child out. If the child doesn't, in the end, answer your question, answer it for the child, "Is that you in the picture? I thought so. Can you say, 'That's me'?"

OFFER SUPPORT FOR THE SAME, DEMANDING WORK

All of this presumes that English language learners are part of the classroom during a writing workshop. These children do not profit from being taken away from the rich language of a reading or a writing workshop in order to work on discrete, out-of-context skills. It is a terrible mistake for an English language learner to practice in the hall with an ELL teacher using flashcards containing colors or seasons while his or her classmates tell and write stories, make explanations, describe, question, reminisce, revise, amplify, clarify, and reach for words to convey meanings. Ideally, ELL teachers should push into classes rather than pulling children out of them.

Some English language learners will come to school not yet proficient in their native language as well as not yet proficient in English. At times, their language proficiency and literacy skills in their first language are not as developed as the language proficiency and literacy skills of the native English speakers at the same grade level. This group of English language learners, then, requires intensive support because not only do they need to develop English language skills, they also need to develop the conceptual knowledge about literacy that has already been developed by many other children their age. These children need extra scaffolding in order to do the rich, complex work of a writing workshop. Too often, instead, they are given low-level tasks such as filling in worksheets. They need just the opposite!

Many English language learners who do not succeed in school are children with undeveloped knowledge of their first language. When these children do not have an extensive vocabulary in their native language, and their conceptual knowledge of literacy has not been sufficiently developed, the process of English language acquisition becomes very complicated. For example, if a child cannot tell time in Spanish, has always told time without using a clock, and yet is expected to learn to tell time from a clock from a teacher speaking in English, this will be tremendously challenging.

These English language learners may need scaffolding in order to do cognitively demanding tasks that involve critical thinking, synthesis, and analysis, but they do not profit from being asked to write lists of words while other children do demanding work without them. A teacher should not avoid using specialized or metaphorical vocabulary in minilessons just because he or she teaches many ELL students, but on the other hand, that teacher will want to provide extra support to ensure that all children can understand what he or she is trying to say. For example, the teacher shouldn't avoid describing an idea as a "watermelon idea" out of fear that the metaphor might confuse English language learners, but the teacher may provide (or ask the ELL teachers to provide) a pre-minilesson in which she says to these children, "Do you know how watermelons are really big? Well, when I say, 'I am thinking of a watermelon idea,' I mean I am thinking of an idea that is as big as a watermelon." In other ways, too, teachers will want to think, "How can I scaffold these children so they can participate in the same intellectually challenging work I envision for other learners?"

PLAN FOR LANGUAGE CHALLENGES

Teachers are also wise to consider the language challenges and the language goals for any unit of study and to deliberately plan for the language curriculum that will be interwoven into the writing curriculum. For example, a teacher working with English language learners can anticipate that writing Small Moment narratives will be challenging for them. It would be easier for these youngsters to write all about a topic than to tell a sequenced story. A teacher working with many ELL students may postpone the Small Moments unit a month, allowing children to write very simple all-about books before shifting into stories, and

she will certainly support oral storytelling from the first day of school. The teacher will probably want to explicitly teach children the sequence/time words that will be important to their work with stories. "When you want to tell what happened in order, you use words like these, 'one day,' 'and then,' 'after that,' and 'finally.'" Of course, the language challenges will be different in different units. When children are writing procedural texts, they will need to use the language of explaining. Again, teachers will want to explicitly teach this language. The teacher might say, "Use words like, 'you need,' 'first you,' 'then you,' and 'don't forget to.'"

When a teacher wants to teach and scaffold children's work with language, it helps to demonstrate and then to give children scaffolded practice. The teacher might say, "If I want to tell someone how to do something, I use words like these: 'First you,' 'then you,' 'after that,' and 'be careful to.' Watch how I teach someone how to put on my shoe, and then I will ask you to teach each other how to put on your shoes." Then the teacher would proceed through the steps, putting her foot into her shoe as she speaks, pointing as she does to the key phrases she will have charted for children. Then she could say, "Now will partner one please tell partner two how you put on your shoe?" When teaching language, it is helpful to invite repetition. Later, you can raise the ante by asking children to teach each other something different—how to zip up their jacket.

These demonstrations often occur in our minilessons, and always it will be important to follow the demonstrations with invitations for children to try what we've just done. The active involvement component of a minilesson becomes especially important when we are working with English language learners.

They need to see and hear us use language, and then they need a chance to have a go with whatever we have shown them. If, for example, I want to teach children about writing strong leads, I might tell the children that sometimes people include the weather or the place in their lead. So "One day I went to the park" becomes, "One sunny day I went to the park." Then I could say, "So tell your friend the story about playing on the monkey bars and start by saying, 'One sunny day.'" I would probably give children repeated active involvements. "Pretend it was a snowy, cold day when you went to the park; tell your partner about that trip to the park." Later I might alter the instructions to give children still more practice. "Now pretend it was a stormy day when you rode your bike." Or, "What if it was night when you rode your bike? Tell your partner how your story might start."

My colleague Amanda Hartman recently led a minilesson designed to teach children how to generate words to accompany a picture. "I have already drawn a picture about when I came in this classroom today. Watch how I point to things in the picture and tell my story," she said. Pointing to the window she had drawn, she said, "It was snowing." Pointing to the picture of the children on the carpet, she added, "The kids were on the carpet. They were smiling." Pointing a stick figure, she said, "I said, 'Good morning.'" After telling her story in this way, she gave each partnership a copy of the picture and asked partner two to point to things and tell the story of her coming into their classroom to partner one. "It was snowing. Our teacher came in. We were all on the rug. We were smiling. . . ." Amanda didn't need to worry that the work she asked children to do was too repetitive. English language learners benefit from repetition.

In order to help English language learners learn from minilessons, it helps to provide visual supports to accompany our oral text. This can mean crystallizing the minilesson into a bare-bones chart that isn't necessarily meant to endure. If I want to remind children of what they can do when they finish a piece, for example, I may suggest five activities, encapsulating each activity in a single word, and then list those words on a chart. It is also helpful for teachers to act out whatever we suggest children try.

When English language learners talk and write, they will make grammatical errors. English language learners often confuse pronouns (he and she) and tenses (writing everything in the present tense even when it should be written in other tenses). They may also have trouble with connectives, using and to link all their sentences. "I ran after her and I was scared and my friend said, 'Watch out,' and I was okay." Once they are past the early production stage, I give them feedback. If the child is talking about his sister and says, "He run," I just say, "Your sister is a girl, so we say 'she runs,' not 'he runs.' Can you say that, 'She runs'?" If the child says, "She runs," and is referring to yesterday, I am apt to say, "It happened yesterday so we say, 'She ran.'" You might add, "Today she runs, yesterday she ran." I definitely want the child to try it. "So can you say that?"

These suggestions for English language learners cannot begin to address the various strengths and needs of each child setting out to learn English. The most important teaching we can offer these children, as all children, is to help them feel like part of the community of literacy learners, with strategies to try in instances of difficulty and people to turn to both when the going gets tough and when it's time to celebrate.

THE LITERACY INSTRUCTION THAT SURROUNDS AND SUPPORTS THE TEACHING OF WRITING

When a school district's educators ask me to assess their writing curriculum, I always say that in order to do so, my visits to the school will need to be long enough for me to understand not only writing instruction itself but also the context for this instruction. The success of a school's writing curriculum relies, in part, on the relationship between the teaching of writing and other aspects of language arts instruction. Ideally, all of the following components are in place.

STORYTELLING

In order for children to write stories, they need to be immersed in a storytelling culture. Too many children don't have opportunities at home to regale their parents with little narratives from their day, nor do they hear parents retelling the funny, sad, or important moments of their lives. It is crucial, then, that schools provide opportunity for children to tell stories to each other, and to hear stories told by authors and teachers and peers.

During even the first few weeks of school, then, we work hard to bring children into a culture of storytelling. For Natalie Louis, the storytelling began with September 11 and the attack on the World Trade Center. When school resumed two days after the attack, Natalie's group of first graders could talk and think of little else. Because there was a fire station across from the school, Natalie's class composed a letter to the firemen. The children were totally involved in the letter, and when they finished writing it they were full of resolve to go, that very instant, to the fire station to deliver it. Natalie was hesitant. She hadn't phoned for an appointment and, anyhow, the firemen might not feel up to having visitors. But her children were adamant and soon they were at the fire station. "If there is a fireman here," Natalie said to the man at the door, "we'd love to deliver a letter to him."

The children waited with bated breath. Then over the loudspeaker they heard, "Brothers, we have guests. Please gather." Firemen in full uniform emerged from all corners and bent low beside the children, quietly waiting while one brave young spokesperson gathered his gumption and delivered a prepared speech and the letter. Then he said, "We have one more thing to give you," and the class tilted back their hands, lifted their eyes, and sang lustily the only song they'd learned that year, "The more we get together. . . ."

When the children convened back in their classroom, Natalie said, "I am never, ever going to forget that trip, are you?" Then she'd added, "What I will do, over and over, is I'll think back on how the visit went. I'm going to remember it *in order*, kind of like I'm telling someone else about it. Let's do that. I'll start." Natalie let the room fill with anticipation. Using her hands to create an imaginary book, she "opened the book" and began. "When we learned that the Twin Towers were attacked and so many firemen died, we knew we needed to do something." She turned an imaginary page, whispering, "Turn the page."

"We wrote our firemen a letter to tell them how we felt. We decided to deliver it." Again, Natalie turned an imaginary page.

"First we lined up in our classroom. Then we walked quietly, quietly down the corridor. . . ." Natalie turned one more page, her voice trailing off, and now Daniel picked up where she had left off, "and we walked down the street and crossed to the fire station."

Natalie whispered, "Turn the page," and turned another page, then looked to see who would speak next. Now Veronica joined in, "We gave them our letter and our song."

The imaginary book frozen in her hands, Natalie said, startled, "Wait! Is that what happened next? Did we cross the street and then give them the letter? Or did something happen first?" Leafing back through a few pages, she said, "Let's turn back a page and try again. Veronica, remember us crossing the street? What happened next?"

Now Veronica said, "We asked the guard if a fireman was there, and he went on the P.A. and said, 'You gotta come.'"

This continued until it was almost time to end the story. "Okay, we're ending soon. Antonio and Jolene, you guys need to end it for us." When they produced, as the ending, "We crossed the street," Natalie "reread" what they'd said with rising intonation which left listeners hanging and signaled that this couldn't *possibly* be the end, could it? "Let's try again," she said, and repeated the last few excerpts, setting Antonio and Jolene up to make an ending. This time, Jolene's last bit was, "and we got back to our classroom."

Nodding in affirmation, Natalie repeated Jolene's ending, slowing the words down so the tone as well as the words created a conclusive wrapping up: "and then, we got back, to—our—classroom." Her eyes sweeping the circle of faces, she added, "We will always remember that day."

Almost every day over the next week or two, Natalie and her class retold this same story. Then they retold it to me when I visited their room. Then they retold it to their principal, embellishing it with new details, adding the candle shrines they'd seen in the fire station and describing the way one fireman slid down the pole.

Another day, Natalie asked her kids to try, at recess, to notice and remember their own little stories. Outside, Natalie watched what children were doing: "Jorge, that adventure you just had on the slide—it's a story! Oh, my gosh! You gotta remember it." Natalie encouraged Jorge to hold the story of the slide in his hand, balled up in his fist. "When we're in the classroom, you can tell the story across your hand," she said, and then opened her hand one digit at a time and began to unfold his story. Opening her thumb, Natalie said, "Your story might go like this."

I stood in the long line for the slide.
(Natalie opened her second finger.)
Finally I got to the top and pushed off.
(Natalie opened the next finger.)
I was sliding down when—Oh, no!—my shoe lace got caught.
(Natalie opened her fourth finger and whispered, "The story is coming to an end soon.")
I pushed. I pulled. I jerked—and suddenly it was free!
(And now one last finger, the end.)
I got to the bottom, safe and sound.

"Remember, it can't be too long, or you'd need ten zillion fingers!" Natalie cautioned.

In all of our classrooms, we have learned the importance of creating a culture where children's stories are valued and told. When New York City extended the length of the school day by fifteen minutes, teachers across Region 8 decided to devote the extra time to storytelling. In these classrooms, the day begins with parents, grandparents, resource room teachers, and specialist teachers all coming into the classroom to sit in small conversation clusters, regaling one another with the story of their lives. In other classrooms, snack time has become an opportunity for children to tell each other the true stories of their lives. When the classroom brims with children's stories, then each child in turn seems to brim with stories. This is the perfect context for a writing workshop.

INTERACTIVE WRITING

Several times a week, the children and teacher work together for ten or fifteen minutes to coauthor a very brief text on the easel. The class, meanwhile, writes the same text on wipe-off boards. This activity allows teachers to highlight features of written language and aspects of the writing process. Depending on what the teacher decides to highlight, children may be reminded to use lowercase letters, to listen for and record blends, to leave spaces between words, to refer to the name chart as a resource, to rely on high frequency words, to use end punctuation, and so forth. I suggest that interactive writing be kept far away from the writing workshop and urge teachers to avoid using interactive writing to provide a story structure for children's own writing. (See the CD-ROM for a detailed transcript of one teacher's interactive writing session.)

THE WORD WALL

Most classrooms will contain an alphabetical display of high frequency words that most of the writers in the class know. Instead of a word wall, some classrooms will feature personal dictionaries full of high frequency words. Either way, the room supports the idea that over time children develop a repertoire of words they "just know." (See the CD-ROM for hints on using a word wall.)

HOME-SCHOOL CONNECTIONS

We know that children will live differently at home because they come to school every day expecting to write. Just as a photographer sees potential photographs everywhere, any time, persons who have time every day to draft, revise, and send out their own important writing projects will see potential topics and purposes for writing in all they do. The predictability of the workshop, then, allows children to live planfully, imagining what they'll do when writing time comes. "Last night I found a quarter in the crack of the sidewalk, and when I came to school I already knew I was going to write about it," Dmitri said.

Hearing this, we celebrate that Dmitri's thinking about writing even when he's not writing. "I do the same thing as a writer," we tell him. "I save up ideas and plan how my text will go. Then the time comes when I can write."

Perhaps on Mondays, homework always includes *writing* (as well as reading, of course), on Tuesdays it may always be science-related, on Wednesdays, homework may always be penmanship, and so forth. By second grade, the writing homework will often entail continuing the writing the children did in school or beginning a new text that will soon travel between home and school (just as children's reading books travel between home and school). But especially after we, as teachers, have met our children's parents at Open House, there will also be writing homework, and a list of suggestions is included in the CD-ROM.

In some schools, each child has a homework buddy. At the start of the day, while children unpack knapsacks and do their jobs, they also meet with their homework buddies to talk about the books they've read the night before and to show each other the other work they've done. The morning sign-in can also include a way to indicate, "I did my homework and checked it with my homework buddy." As part of morning sign-in, each child can learn to transfer his or her homework into the appropriate folder. In the case of writing, each child transfers his or her writing from the homework file to the child's work-in-progress writing folder.

PHONEMIC AWARENESS AND PHONICS

The term *phonemic awareness* refers to the ability to blend sounds together to form spoken words and the ability to break spoken words into their constituent sounds. Phonemic awareness is necessary in order for children to use their letter-sound knowledge as they read and write. Phonemic awareness is the beginning of literacy.

Although most of us teachers learned to read and write without any special instruction in phonemic awareness, a group of researchers have recently found that children who end up struggling as readers and writers sometimes do so because they never developed this foundation for future graphophonic

work. Most children develop phonemic awareness from language play and from opportunities to read and write. But some children don't have these opportunities, or have these opportunities but need more explicit help. Because we don't necessarily know which child will need what support, teachers are encouraged to plan for and teach a bit of phonemic awareness in kindergarten and first grade. Reading researchers who emphasize the importance of phonemic awareness still suggest that kindergarten teachers spend a total of only twenty hours, spread across the year, teaching phonemic awareness (and less time in first grade). This works out to between five and seven minutes of phonemic awareness per day! (Natalie Louis's description of how she supports phonemic awareness in her children is available on the CD-ROM.)

The term *phonics* refers to sound-letter correspondences and to children's abilities to word solve as readers and as writers. Often, teachers structure the phonics component of their curriculum rather like a reading or a writing workshop, with an explicit minilesson followed by time for children to work independently, with partners, or in small groups with the teacher coaching them. In a phonics lesson, children are explicitly taught something, perhaps information about sound-letter correspondence, rimes, spelling patterns, contractions, possessives, or the like. Then children use this explicit teaching in multilevel activities. For example, the teacher may teach a rime—perhaps *op*—and then children may work in partnerships to generate lists of words that contain that particular sound. Some lists will include *operation* and *helicopter*; others will be filled with one-syllable rhymes such as *mop, pop,* and *top.* The day's lesson ends with either a teaching share or another closure activity.

An Interactive Read-Aloud with Accountable Talk, Children's Literature

Over the course of each day, teachers read aloud several times for a range of purposes. On most days, one of the read-alouds is an interactive read-aloud, with children talking in response to it, using accountable talk to develop ideas that are grounded in the text and in the conversation.

The classroom needs to brim with the best of children's literature and with a reverence for literature. This is shown by the way books are featured around the room—as part of a science center, displayed along the chalk tray—and it is also evident in the care with which books are treated. Is there a hospital for damaged books? A special display for brand-new books? The library area, too, needs to be treated with respect. Ideally, children feel as if they are on a first-name basis with a few writers whom they know well.

Shared Reading

Young children need experience doing reading work together with an experienced reader. Students reading together with the teacher is called *shared reading*. During this time of the day, all eyes are on one shared text, and students can feel what it is like to read; they can get one step closer to being able to practice reading on their own. Buoyed by the support of the classroom reading community, children experience what it is to function like strong readers and, meanwhile, learn to integrate the skills and strategies that constitute reading as they experience a text together. During this time, we teach children to read class songs, big books, texts we've written together, and other writing that eventually becomes familiar to our students.

Independent, Partner, and Guided Reading

It is crucial that a child have at least thirty minutes a day to read as best he or she can. In kindergarten, much of the reading children do will be reading with training wheels of one sort of another. That is, children will reread texts they know from shared reading, they'll read very supportive texts with the help of a book introduction, or they'll reread rich storybooks they know well, relying more on the pictures and on their memory of the text. As this happens, we teach children to become conventional readers.

Teachers bring together small groups of children who need similar support, teach a particular strategy, and set children up to use that strategy on the run as they read a text. Then the teacher watches them read and intervenes to coach the readers.

CHOICE TIME: DRAMATIC PLAY

Every expert of early childhood knows the centrality of play in a child's education. Every quality that we admire in learners— tenacity, resourcefulness, curiosity, an ability to cooperate with others, expressive and flexible language—can be developed most easily by children's play. Dramatic play is especially potent to a child's literacy development, because in dramatic play the child creates alternate worlds and lets characters come to life in those worlds. Is this not at the heart of all reading and writing?

SPELLING AND THE PRIMARY WRITING WORKSHOP

It is crucial to teach children to approximate, spell the best they can, and keep going. If you don't, most of the class will spend most of their day waiting for you to do their spelling for them. If you let children recruit you into doing the work for them, everyone in the class will spend a lot of time waiting passively (or rambunctiously) while you rush about providing spellings.

If your children won't stop begging for spelling help, if you find yourself saying, "But my kids keep asking for me to spell words. What do I do?" then you haven't clearly conveyed to them that they need to approximate and keep going. Your children only keep asking because you keep providing. If your message is consistent and clear, children will soon learn to carry on as best they can. This means that whenever a child in the midst of spelling asks for help, it's wise to say, "Do the best you can and keep going," or "Say it slowly and write down what you hear," or "What do you know that can help you with that word?" Remember that children learn from their own efforts and that they'll gain more from working to write *mommy* and getting the word partly right and partly wrong than from you providing the perfect spelling.

When children are just learning about letter-sound connections, they need to know that when they are trying to spell a word, one of the first things to do is stretch the word out, breaking it into component sounds and recording the sounds they hear. Very soon, however, children need to rely on visual memory of the word and to use words they know to help with words they don't know how to spell. English words contain many letters that don't directly correspond to sounds, and children who struggle with spelling are often children who remain phonetic spellers. It's wise to have a consistent cross-grade whole-school approach to spelling and to organize this around the goal of helping all children develop the strategies that good spellers use. Never, ever say, "Spelling doesn't matter." That's not a wise message. Instead, say, "When you are writing and you don't know how to spell a word, try it; do your best and keep going."

ASSESSMENT

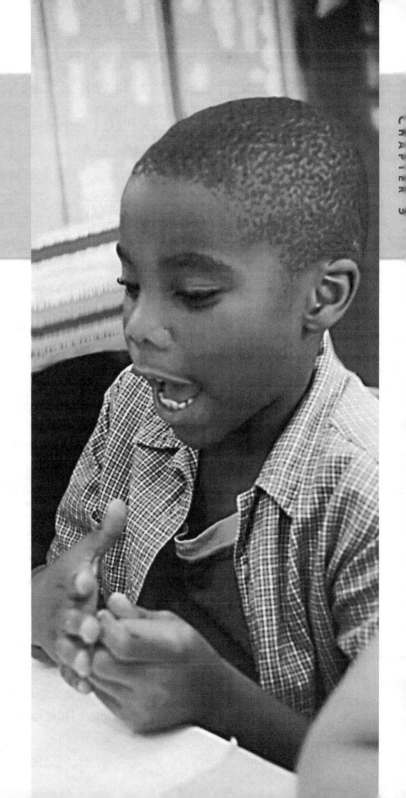

A writer puts marks on the page and we, as teachers of writing, read the writing and we read the writer. We read as a reader, responding to the heartache and adventure, humor and information that the child has encoded onto the page, laughing and gasping and inquiring in response to what we find there. We also read as a teacher of writing, noticing what the child has tried to do and has done and can almost do.

In the teaching my colleagues and I have described, assessment occurs in little and big ways throughout every minute of our teaching. As a school year unfurls, it is not only our curriculum but also our assessments that change.

Assessment That Informs Us as We Develop a Curricular Calendar

Toward the end of one school year or the start of the summer, when teachers across a grade level—or a lone teacher, if need be—devote extended time to planning the upcoming year's curricular calendar, it is crucial to begin by assessing the year that is ending and the work our departing students have done during that year. We will want to reflect on our teaching, on the work our students have done, and on the progress our students have (and have not) made. We do all this with an eye toward growing new curricular plans for the year ahead.

▸ **What worked?** Did my teaching feel especially vital and strong during particular units of study? What made it work then? How can I build on this so that more of my teaching feels this way in the year ahead?

▸ **What didn't work?** Where did my teaching feel as if it was floundering? What lessons can be drawn from that? How can I make curricular (and other) plans for the year ahead so that my teaching gets stronger? Should I tackle different units of study? Secure more support for particular units of study? Develop my own muscles for teaching particular things? What game plan could I develop that might help me outgrow myself?

▸ **What have students learned?** In looking over my students' written products, what have almost all of my students learned to do as a result of my teaching? How can I be sure

to provide next year's students with these same opportunities—and help next year's students go even farther?

▸ **What do students need to learn?** In what ways could my students' work be dramatically strengthened? Obviously, it will take more than curricular plans to strengthen student work, but how can I design units of study that will help to take students on the journey I have in mind for them?

Assessment That Informs Us as We Plan for the First Days of School

Summer has a way of slipping away quickly, and all of a sudden the new year is upon us, with a host of new children. It is crucial for us to make real contact with each and every child as fast as we possibly can. Children need to come into our classroom and feel seen and heard. They need this instantly—all of them do. How helpful it is if we give ourselves a head start!

Toward the end of the preceding year, many schools organize what some people call "up and down" visits. The second-grade teachers spend a week (or a day) teaching in the first grade, the first-grade teachers spend similar time teaching in kindergarten, and the kindergarten teachers meanwhile visit feeder preschools. Ideally, these visits happen while the host teacher is in the classroom, but in some schools, every teacher rotates, each teacher teaching the incoming grade for a few days (following the teaching plans of the host teacher) and in this way learning the norms and expectations for the upcoming children. This means that in September, teachers can deliberately create consistency. Teachers can remind children of what they were able to do at the end of the preceding year, and convey the message that that will be the starting point for the new year. This makes a world of difference, because all too often teachers' expectations for their class do not carry children along a thoughtful gradient of difficulty. For example, children may be writing six-page books at the end of first grade, then move on to second-grade teachers who ask them to merely draw and write a few sentences under the picture!

Some teachers find it helps to write children's parents a letter in the summer. "I know my teaching will be strongest if I connect with your child as quickly as I can. Could you take a few minutes to write and tell me about your son? Tell me about his passions and his worries; tell me about his friendships and his family. What does he like to do when he has a free day?"

Assessment must occur continually as we teach writing. The child does something—anything—and we, as teachers think, "What is this child showing me? What might the child be trying to do? Able to do? What seems to be just beyond the child's independent grasp?" The child acts, and the teacher interprets those actions and thinks, "How can I best respond?"

The challenge in writing a chapter on assessment, then, is that assessment happens in so many ways, for so many purposes, that it is hard to pin down. Assessment is the thinking teacher's mind work. It is the intelligence that guides our every moment as a teacher.

GUIDING PRINCIPLES FOR ASSESSMENT

When we, as teachers, assess a child as a writer, we try to discern what the child can do independently so that we can determine the next step for this child. Just as readers benefit if teachers help them progress along a gradient of difficulty so that they sometimes receive the necessary help to read books that are just a tiny bit beyond their independent reach, so too writers need instruction that scaffolds them to extend what they can do just one notch further. The pathways in Chapter 2 suggest one trail along which writers develop, but there are lots of lines of growth for writers, and a skilled teacher can note what a child is doing and could, with help, be able to do along any one of a great many lines of growth.

For example, the teacher can look at a child's ability to organize non-narrative writing. Can the child write in topic-based subcategories so that information on "feeding my dog" is in a different place than information on "training my dog"? If the child can do this, can the child organize the information within any one sub-category according to some principle? Is there some logic—any logic—informing the sequence of information in a section on "feeding my dog," for example?

Teachers of writing need to be able to look at a piece of writing with a particular growth line in mind, name what the child can do along that growth line, and imagine what a logical next step might be. This assessment is necessary in order for the teacher to provide children with the scaffolds they need to develop as writers. What the child can do at one moment with support, the child should be able to do at another moment with independence.

It is important for teachers to realize that assessments will be more useful if, at any one time, we deliberately choose the lens through which we look. If we don't consciously make this choice, we probably apply different criteria to different children. That is, without even realizing we are doing so, we may end up looking at the strong writers' work with an eye toward organization and looking at less experienced writers' work with eyes only on spelling and penmanship. Of course, there are countless possible lenses that teachers could look through in order to view their students as writers. How are children doing at spelling sight words correctly? At controlling lowercase and uppercase letters? At writing story endings? At producing a lot of work? At getting started writing without needing a personal nudge? At rereading their own work? At writing with detail?

It is probably a worthwhile endeavor to sometimes look over the entire class, thinking, "How are all my children doing at any one of the areas cited above?" For example, a teacher could ask, "How are all my children doing at writing stories in which a character moves sequentially through time?" This will probably result in the teacher gathering clusters of children together and providing each cluster with some small-group strategy lessons.

If assessments are going to inform instruction, then it is crucial that a teacher understand that the question is always "What can a child do now?" and "What can a child almost do now?" The question "What can't a child do?" doesn't tend to inform instruction, because there will always be vast terrain that is beyond any learner. Just because a child can't synthesize information from six sources or write citations with correct footnotes does not mean that this is what we should teach the child! But if we discern that the child makes characters inside his drawing speak in speech balloons but has never yet made characters inside the text of his story speak, then it is logical to speculate that we could perhaps show this child how to bring the contents of those speech balloons into the body of his story. In this fashion, then, the job of assessment involves finding the growing tip of a child's writing development and nurturing it.

When one is learning a skill, it's great fun to see oneself getting better. Whether learning to play softball or to swim or to roller-skate, it helps to have concrete goals and to be able to see and record one's progress toward those goals. The fledgling swimmer works hard to swim from one side of the pool to the other. When the child meets this goal, he is ready for the next goal. Again, the child will work hard en route to the new goal.

Writing development occurs on lots of fronts, and children can't consciously tackle all the goals that a teacher has in mind, but it is helpful for the child to have a palpable, concrete sense of what good work entails and to be able to chart his or her progress toward at least some fairly obvious aspects of that goal. This means that it is important to show children examples of good work that are within the child's reach and to supply children with guidelines they can apply when assessing their own work.

It is also important that children join with teachers in noticing the pathway they've already traveled and in setting goals for the next phase of their development. This sort of frank discussion should occur often in a conference. "I see you are able to do this now and that is great—what I think you need to reach toward now is this. Let me help you get started doing that with me nearby to help. Okay, now see if you can keep going without me. Wow! You did it! From now on, do this whenever you write."

Whenever educators assess what the children to whom we are responsible know and can do as writers, it is important that we understand that the children are providing us with mirrors. We can look at the children's work and see ourselves and learn from the effectiveness of our work with the children. Whether the assessor is the classroom teacher, the building principal, or the involved staff developer, we need to understand that the information about what our children can and cannot do as writers is also information about what we have and have not done in our perspective roles. What have we done well? What must we begin to do better? What could be the sources of trouble? How could we best respond? The most valuable assessment will always be self-assessment.

People learn as much or more from attention to growth and celebrations of progress as from critique.

TOOLS FOR ASSESSMENT

When we teach writing, the good news is that children regularly give us demonstrations of what they know and can do. The first step toward becoming a teacher who assesses children's writing is being sure that each child has one folder containing his or her recent work and a different portfolio containing samples of work accumulated across the year or even across several years.

When considering which work deserves to be saved, the most important thing is to save the work that children themselves have produced. That is, there are lots of reasons to edit, word-process, and publish children's writing, but for the purpose of assessment, the writing that really needs to be dated, organized, saved, and studied is the rough drafts of what children themselves have written.

The first tool for assessment, then, is the writing folder—all of a child's writing accumulated within a unit of study, with some of that work going home only after the unit of study has ended. At this time, some work is selected for the child's cumulative portfolio.

It is also important that teachers and children work toward clearly specified goals within a unit of study and across the year. The curriculum that is contained within this series of books has been designed to help all students reach the rigorous goals outlined by the New Primary Literacy Standards published by the National Center on Education and the Economy (see www.ncee.org). Of course, end-of-the-year standards need to inform the day-to-day decisions we make every day as we teach. To that end, we have specified clear goals for each unit of study, and this helps us assess each child and our own

		1	2	3	4	5
Attitude	The child approaches writing with eagerness and confidence, conveying the impression that he finds writing doable and worth doing. He may not write with conventional spelling or even with alphabet letters, but he does write with confidence and enthusiasm. He shares his writing with confidence and expects others to study his marks with interest in their content.					
Planning	The child generates ideas for writing without resistance or difficulty. He uses drawing as a placeholder to hold his ideas and as rehearsal for the text he plans to write (or tell).					
Independence	The child works with independence and initiative in the writing workshop. On many days he moves from the whole group to his writing place, selects appropriate paper, secures utensils, settles into work on the page, and carries on with initiative and independence for at least 15 to 20 minutes.					
	The child persists in his work for longer stretches of time. When he finishes one piece of writing, he begins the next without missing a beat or needing a teacher's intervention. He has progressed from regarding a piece of writing as a one-day proposition. By now, the child often staples or tapes more paper onto the original page, letting his initial story grow.					
Purpose	The child knows that writing is a way to communicate meaning. The child uses the writing workshop as a time to pay attention and share the details of his life. He approaches writing using any means possible—drawing, written words, accompanied oral commentary—to capture that meaning. That is, the child does not regard writing as primarily an opportunity to display his prowess with print (thereby resorting to copying or listing known words).					
Genre	There has been no direct instruction in genre. The child will probably tell about a topic or retell an event.					
Productivity	The child works productively every day during the writing workshop so that by the end of this unit, he has produced a large stack of at least 30 pages of work, with most pages containing either fairly detailed drawings and/or a more sketchy drawing plus sentences of print. His pages show engagement, activity, and persistence.					
Graphophonics	The child knows that during writing time he must write words as best he can. He at least knows that a writer says the word slowly, listening for the sounds, and records the sounds he hears. (He may know about other strategies such as relying on known words, visual knowledge, familiar chunks, etc.) The child works to do his best to write and spell; he may do any one of the following: • The child makes writing-like marks that show a growing knowledge of concepts of print. They go left to right, top to bottom, contain alphabet letters, etc. • The child labels items in the drawing, mostly using initial consonants. If the child hears a sound but doesn't know the letter that matches the sound, he either approximates as best he can or solicits help from a peer. The child may or may not also write strings of letters on lines at the bottom of pages, but he does generate and tell a rich oral story to accompany the drawing. With help from others, the child hears more sounds, so his labels will soon contain more than a single letter. • The child labels items with more than initial sounds. He will, with help, soon write a sentence under each picture (as well as perhaps continuing to write labels on his drawings). • The child writes a sentence under his picture. The letters are not random, but they may appear to be because various things (no spaces between words, limited sound-letter knowledge, few high frequency words) make the writing difficult to read. The child learns, with help, to leave spaces between words and to provide readers with more letters, so that his writing becomes easier to read. • The child writes in a way that is conventional enough that together he and the teacher can often reread the text. The child rereads, with urging and help, while monitoring for one-to-one matching, revising to make the actual text more closely match the intended text.					
Writing Process	The child can work through portions of the writing process with independence (generating topics, planning writing, envisioning a subject, recording it on the page) and can work through other portions of the process with adult help (rereading what he has written and adding on).					
Qualities of Good Writing	The child's writing shows his understanding of what it means to write well. The teacher can learn this also by asking the child to select his best piece(s): "What makes this better than the others?" "If you were to improve this, what might you do?"					
Language	The child joins in opportunities for storytelling. These may occur across the day.					
Reading	The child knows how to listen to and enjoy the teacher's reading aloud. The child can tell where on the page the type is found and what its function is.					

This rubric can also be found on the CD-ROM Resources for Primary Writing.

teaching within each unit with an eye toward whether children are meeting these unit-by-unit goals. These incremental goals are aligned with end-of-the-year standards. The same organizing terms and values inform both the unit-by-unit goals and the standards. You'll find rubrics (such as the one shown on page 88) in each unit of study; all of them are on the CD-ROM of resources.

Although assessment weaves through every moment of our teaching, we especially assess during one-to-one writing conferences. For many years, teachers in our community carried clipboards with them while conferring and scrawled anecdotal notes about the child's topic, genre, and process decisions. Recently, however, we studied those anecdotal notes and found that sometimes the expectation that we must keep records during our conferences distracts teachers from feeling duty-bound to teach the child something during these interactions. We can find ourselves dutifully recording whatever the child says in a conference and then moving on, oblivious to the fact that we have taught the child nothing. In order to make it more likely that our conferences actually provide teaching opportunities, we have recently begun speculating in advance on the sort of things we will watch for in order to see what children do. We watch with a conferring record sheet in hand, and if children do something we regard as significant to the unit, we mark off that the child has done whatever we observed. If we teach the child a particular skill or strategy, then we record a T for teaching and then hope that in the days ahead we'll observe (and record) the child doing this independently. In this way, our record sheet of the conferences we hold with individuals also records what individual writers are able to do. You'll find checklist such as the

following in each of the units of study; all the unit checklists are also on the CD-ROM.

Assessment is not an end in itself. Assessment must be purposeful to be either effective or useful. Our notes and files can't stay in the drawer or on the shelf gathering dust, or they have been for naught. They need to be brought into the public eye at times, to show what children can learn to do when given the chance. They are the evidence that allows us to teach in the ways we know are best for children. These static assessment files have their purpose in allowing us to be held accountable to others and ourselves for our teaching work. But changing, growing assessment notes are most useful to our teaching and learning. When we take what we learn about our students from assessment and use that information to teach them more or differently, to place them in helpful learning contexts, and to show them how their hard work has made a difference in their ability to make sense of and participate in the world, then our assessment has truly been worthy of us and worthy of our students.

Assessment Checklist for *Launching the Writing Workshop*

T - taught
O - must teach soon
/ - saw evidence that writer can do
X - saw more evidence that writer can do

Names

Goals

Category	Goal											
Attitude	Writer generates topics without resistance.											
	Writer assumes the identity of "I'm an author!"											
Planning	Writer chooses paper that is appropriate.											
	Writer makes the transition from the minilesson to writing.											
Independence	Writer cycles through the process with independence, starting a new piece when the last is done.											
Genre	Writer's text conveys either a story or information.											
Purpose	Writer knows writing conveys meaning. He creates coherent oral (or written) text to accompany pictures.											
Productivity	Writer is socialized into the norms and mores of a writing workshop, carrying on productively for 20–30 minutes.											
	Writer's marks show growing concepts of print (top to bottom, alphabet letters, etc.).											
	Writer writes labels, sentences, or stories using sound-letter correspondence, etc., to do so.											
Graphophonics	Writer has strategies for spelling unfamiliar words (at least stretches out a word, then hears and records initial or dominant sound).											
	Writer revises by adding details into pictures/text and by adding more pages to text.											
Writing Process	Writer uses resources appropriately to help with spelling.											
	Writer tries to make his marks on the page match his mental image.											
Qualities of Good Writing	Writer talks about the value of details.											
Reading	Writer identifies print and understands its function in different texts.											

This checklist can also be found on the CD-ROM Resources for Primary Writing.